THE
ASTRO-LUNA
JOURNAL

Journey with the Moon and the 12 astrological archetypes to deepen your understanding, support inner development, and get in tune with natural cycles.

Written by Monika Anna
Illustrated by Sibylline Meynet

LIMINAL 11

First published in 2022 by Liminal 11

Words copyright © 2022 Monika Anna
Images copyright © 2022 Sibylline Meynet

Cover Design: Allie Oldfield
Designers: Allie Oldfield and Tori Jones
Editor: Eleanor Tremeer
Editorial Director: Darren Shill
Artistic Director: Kay Medaglia

Printed in Malaysia

ISBN 978-1-912634-41-5

10 9 8 7 6 5 4 3 2 1

www.liminal11.com

TABLE OF CONTENTS

PERSONAL INVITATION

Welcome to *The Astro-Luna Journal*, and thank you for joining this adventure.

I invite you on a journey with the Moon and her phases, to travel through all 12 star signs and learn about the zodiac's archetypal energies and cycles. You will do this by journaling throughout the year, keeping track of your feelings with each New and Full Moon phase as they appear on the backdrop of every star sign. It is through the language of astrology, which in symbolic ways describes our desires and fears, that you will learn more about your inner and outer worlds. In this adventure, you will examine your connections with the Moon and work with your inner rhythm to experience a world that is more connected than you might think.

As with so many adventures, I'd love this one to be fun, unpredictable, challenging at times, full of discoveries, new friends, and – most importantly – worth your while. As the Moon reflects the light of the Sun, in this journal I encourage you to find the reflection of your inner light in the world around you. To begin, all you need is an open mind and a willingness to try new things, as well as time to observe, to reflect, to meditate and to journal.

This journey will be different to all those taken before because you are not going to go from point A to B. You won't follow a straight path and many of us won't even start in the same place. What I truly hope is that you will arrive at a place of deeper understanding, of a stronger connection with your own body, with your own life, and with your own soul.

You are a wonder and a miracle. I'd love for you to rediscover this magic within you; to remember all the parts of yourself that are so special, strong, creative and subtle, and to collect them one by one as you go through this introspection. My hope is this journey will transform your life in a unique and meaningful way.

HOW TO USE THIS BOOK

This book was created to support you in getting in touch with the energies of the cosmos, as well as your internal cycles; to help you understand the language of the stars locked in the symbolism of the 12 zodiac archetypes; and to use the Moon's cycle to reconnect with your body's natural rhythm.

Each month at the New Moon, you will read about the symbolism of its specific zodiac sign (i.e. Aquarius) and meditate on how it manifests in your life. You'll have space to set up an intention for the month ahead and write affirmations to help you stay connected to this symbolism throughout the month. Also, a few helpful questions will support your journaling on the themes linked with that sign, to deepen your understanding.

At the Full Moon, you'll learn about another aspect of zodiac energy (i.e. Leo) and practice gratitude with some helpful journal prompts. You'll have space to reflect on how those astrological archetypes are manifesting in the world around you. As you work with this book, you'll be able to look back not only to the beginning of the monthly cycle (i.e. New Moon in Aquarius) but also to the beginning of the cycle that started six months before (i.e. New Moon in Leo). Having a record of your intimate thoughts and intentions to look back on will support you in this adventure.

This book will strengthen your practice of mindfulness and self-care by helping you create a sacred space of reflection while deepening your understanding of the natural cycles. It is here for you to have fun, to dream, to slow down. Most importantly, this journal will help you return to a state of interconnectedness and to see the world and yourself as they truly are – magical and enchanting.

As we go into cyclical timing there is no need for a structured diary. We won't be starting on the 1st of January, because any New Moon is a new beginning. It does not matter when you pick up this journal or even if you take a break. Start where you are. What's your nearest New Moon? Start there, because it's the journey that matters, not the destination.

Let us begin!

WHAT YOU NEED TO PREPARE FOR THIS ADVENTURE:

◆ A pen or pencil.

◆ Time set aside for reflection, meditation and journaling

◆ A phone app or almanack with dates of the Moon phases and the zodiac signs they are passing through

As with any journey, our Luna's adventure can begin with small steps. I invite you to start by taking five minutes each day to orientate yourself. Where is the Moon in the sky? Is she waning or waxing? Knowing her rhythm will bring you closer to two pivotal points in her journey – the New and Full Moon phases.

YOUR BIRTH CHART – GOING DEEPER AND MORE PERSONAL:

You do not need to know your personal astrological information in order to use *The Astro-Luna Journal*. However, to go deeper and examine your internal cycles, you can use information from your birth chart.

Your personal horoscope is based on the date, time and place of your birth, and provides a range of information you can use. It tells you the Moon phase that you were born under, which describes your emotional characteristics, who you are in the world, and how you nurture yourself and others. Are you a New Moon baby, full of enthusiasm, or a Crescent Moon, working through difficulties? Astrological houses in your chart provide information about various areas of life, which are highlighted by the transit of the Moon.

Your birth chart shows a combination of zodiac signs and astrological houses which are unique to you. Houses in astrology describe different areas of our existence. For example, the fourth house is about family and our roots, the sixth house is about day-to-day routines and health, the seventh house talks about relationships, etc. As the Moon passes through the zodiac, she will shine her light into the house connected with that sign, so if you use your birth chart while you journal, you can see which sphere of life will be activated on the New and Full Moon.

Knowing how each Moon phase affects your chart will make your journal more meaningful and customized to you – and will help you see bigger patterns reflected in specific areas of your life. A quiet reflection at the New Moon and expressing gratitude at the Full Moon will deepen your relationship with the cosmos and will show you how intimately and uniquely you are linked with it.

TO GET YOUR BIRTH CHART:

You'll need your date, time and place of birth to create a free birth chart. (See appendix for a list of free websites that will calculate this for you.) Your birth chart will show your rising sign (or Ascendant), which is also the cusp of your first house.

CHAPTER GUIDE

VOL I

Here you will find information to help you prepare for your journal.

Moon Phases And Their Energy

In this chapter, you will learn about the eight Moon phases and how they are linked with eight annual Sun festivals. What do they have in common, what energy do they bring and how can you work with them?

Creating Your Moon Ritual

I'll introduce you to the concept of rituals and reflect on why we need them in our lives at times of transition and change. There will also be guidance on how you can create a New and Full Moon ritual to help you get the most out of this journal.

VOL II

This is the main part of the journal and where the magic happens!

The 12 Heavenly Archetypes

You'll be introduced to the concept of polarity, modality and elements within the zodiac signs. This provides an extra layer of understanding of the signs and can help when planning your rituals.

Your Astro-Luna Journal

This is the journal itself, where you can record how the different Moon phases affect your life. For each of the 12 zodiac signs, you will have:

✦ A short description of each archetype.

✦ An explanation of how each archetype is affected by each Moon phase.

✦ Info about attributes and keywords to help with journaling.

The journal includes:

◆ Space for the date, and, if you wish, an astrological degree and house placement.

◆ Space to write your affirmation, based on the keywords provided, to act as a guide through the cycles.

◆ Space to set your intention and vision for the Moon cycle, based on the symbolism of that Moon phase and the sign it falls into.

◆ Three engaging questions to inspire your journaling and open up your awareness.

In the Full Moon section, you have extra space to reflect on the beginning of the cycle, so you can refer back to the previous New Moon (two weeks before) or the last New Moon in the same sign as the current Full Moon (six months before). This will help you review the wishes you planted at the time, and consider how that sign's energy is culminating in the current Full Moon.

VOL III

Includes extra information for your journey with the Moon in the journal and beyond.

Mansions In The Sky

This chapter covers the houses of the horoscope, their fundamental meanings and how to find yours in the birth chart. It also gives a short interpretation of how the New and Full Moon energies can manifest in those areas, so you can use this section as a reference point to deepen your Moon ritual and journaling.

Your Personal Moon

Through the pages of this journal, you will have embarked on your adventure with the Moon in the sky and her travel through all 12 zodiac signs. In this section, I will introduce you to the concept of the internal Moon and the soul journey, so you can work with energies without and within and find a more holistic and balanced approach to your life.

Welcome to your introduction to Moon phases and ritual.

This volume invites you to reflect on what it means to have sacred
space in your life. How do you create it in a practical, physical way
and on a more subtle, spiritual plane? As you construct your own
personal New and Full Moon ritual, you are preparing yourself for
a transformational experience...

MOON PHASES AND THEIR ENERGY

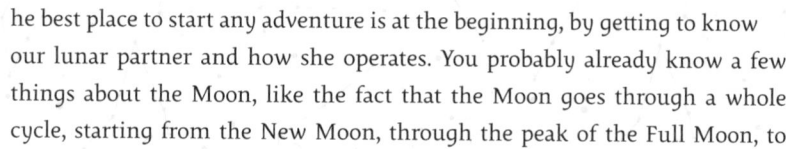

The best place to start any adventure is at the beginning, by getting to know our lunar partner and how she operates. You probably already know a few things about the Moon, like the fact that the Moon goes through a whole cycle, starting from the New Moon, through the peak of the Full Moon, to the end of that cycle and a new beginning at the next New Moon. This whole journey takes approximately 28 days. You might also already be familiar with the fact that, throughout that time, the Moon appears in the sky in eight different phases. To work with this ever-changing energy, we need to get even more familiar with the meaning behind it.

The Moon phase cycle is really a Moon and Sun cycle. It's the dance that the Moon, Earth and Sun perform each month as they circle around each other. Without the life-giving light of the Sun, there would be no reflection on the surface of the Moon, and without the dance with Earth, there would be no visible phases. As the Moon whirls around the Earth and receives the Sun's illuminating light, it appears to us differently depending on her position. This rhythm and ebb and flow of the energy are constant, but the quality of it changes every month, as the Moon starts her journey in a different sign of the zodiac. Throughout the year, she will begin her cycle in all 12 star signs.

The Sun cycle, called "The Wheel of the Year" by pagans, refers to eight Sun festivals throughout the year. You don't have to be religious or spiritual to acknowledge the Sun's journey. Our Sun goes through changes and we follow his progress through the depths of night and darkness in the winter, through the warm rays in spring that thaw our Earth, to the height of summer heat. Those eight festivals acknowledge specific stations in this pilgrimage.

Elders of many traditions understood this cycle and our connection with the life-giving force of the Sun and incorporated them into their own beliefs and religious customs. Many traditions around the world carry the wisdom that teaches us about this internal clock and knowledge about specific times and seasons for everything in life. These days, most of the world's population lives in artificially lit urban areas, and we spend a significant amount of our time in schools, offices or houses with light-on-demand, so the cycle of light and darkness is disrupted.

Given how disconnected we are from the very visible Sun cycle, it's no surprise that the more subtle and quicker Moon cycle is getting missed too. Both are intricately connected and intertwined. Those who work closely with nature still work with this natural clock. Life is in constant ebb and flow, and our planting and harvesting still respond not only to the time of the year in the Sun cycle, but also the time of the month and the Moon cycle. As humans, we are not immune to this either. With our internal circadian rhythm, the light and darkness, the Sun and Moon's influence play a part in our own wellbeing, too.

Because of this interconnectedness of both our luminaries, the monthly Moon and yearly Sun cycle have a lot of similarities. We can therefore compare the energy of each Moon phase to one of the eight Sun festivals. To understand them more deeply, we can compare them as a cycle within a cycle, spinning endlessly within the Wheel of the Year...

DARK PHASES AND WINTER

New Moon / Yule – Winter Solstice
During the New Moon, the spirit is pulling us within. Once a month, we are compelled to slow down, to preserve our energy, to dream the dreams of the future on the night of no Moon. This is a time of planting seeds of new beginnings, which will be born of our intuition and inner impulses in the coming Crescent phase. It's a time of reconnecting with the invisible, with the inmost, with our roots, our ancestry, our dreams, and our stories. This is a time when the seed of our dream cannot see the light and it dreams of awakening, buried deep in the womb of our creative souls.

This Moon phase can be linked with the winter solstice in the Northern Hemisphere, which is the longest night of the year, and marks the beginning of the new Sun cycle. The Sun is at its weakest point; there is much less heat to warm our Earth; there is not enough light to help vegetation grow and flourish. We are surrounded by darkness and we, and nature around us, tend to gravitate inwards – inside our houses, inside ourselves. It's the time of hibernation, so we don't expend too much of the life force offered by the Sun. It's the time of preservation of the creative spirit, concentrating on going deep within and evaluating our strengths and weaknesses in the long hours of the night. It's the time of connecting with our most inner voice and weaving the dream and vision that will be released into the future.

Waxing Crescent / Imbolc

Three to four days after the New Moon we have the Waxing Crescent phase. The Moon is finally clearly visible in the sky and our Luna returns to the heavens with her crescent bow. The seed of our vision that we planted at the New Moon has cracked its shell and is now pushing through with all the strength that it has. The first shoots of dreams emerge and begin to see the light and the journey ahead.

The Waxing Crescent Moon gives us foresight into the journey ahead. We have a vision, which came through the time of deep communion with our inner self, and now that vision is getting focused and directed, so that it can blossom in time. This is the Moon phase that takes a lot of energy and strength from us, as we need to break through and see the hope for our dreams. This is the moment of first, bold steps and actions, taken with all the vigor and enthusiasm that we can muster. This is the time of finding the inner strength to break through any obstacles.

The Waxing Crescent phase has a similar energy to Imbolc and Candlemas, which are only two names of many for this Sun festival. They all acknowledge the return of the light. After long nights of winter months, around the time of Imbolc, we can visibly see days getting longer and the light getting stronger. It's not a concept anymore, but a reality that we can observe. It's faint and weak, but the hope for a new life is being born with that light, and with it the promise of future growth and abundance. It is the promise of the summer days to come and of life returning to its power; the promise of life and survival after the scarcity and harshness of winter.

LIGHT ASCENDING AND SPRING

First Quarter / Ostara – Spring Equinox

The First Quarter Moon is the crisis point that challenges us to recommit to what we want to blossom at the Full Moon. With so much energy and effort already exerted, and as we are only halfway to our goal, this is the moment of confrontation. We are faced with an uphill battle and we are asked whether we have the commitment and endurance to reach our goal. We are challenged to dig even deeper than before, to take risks that will strengthen our position. This is the time of commitment to our vision, of overcoming obstacles and showing the courage of our convictions, so determination can help us push forward.

The spring equinox brings harmony between light and dark: the night is now balanced by day, and the light has just won the battle with the darkness as the days are now growing longer. From this moment on, the Sun is stronger. The spring equinox lights a fire in us and the fight for life, for survival, must take place. We must reconfirm our pledge to the light both in the world and inside us, to push further and overcome the shadow within.

Waxing Gibbous / Beltane

Waxing Gibbous energy concerns perfecting and improving our vision, just before it bursts with the energy of the Full Moon. After the crisis and recommitting to the dream in the first quarter of the Moon's cycle, we can now almost taste success. This is the last moment of growth, of corrections, of enrichment, of enhancement before completion. These are the last moments of nourishment that we can offer. It's the time of maturation, and time for last-minute improvements and final touches.

We have similar energy at Beltane, when the world is full of potential. The buds are forming, and the fruits are growing – we can sense the heat of summer days approaching. The anticipation of the fullness of life and preparation for the peak of the phase at summer solstice gets us all excited. The fresh fragrance in the air is intoxicating with the promise of the eruption of life and the ecstasy of nature in full bloom. Nature is energized and ready to take the last few steps before the crowning of the Sun.

HEIGHT OF THE CYCLE AND SUMMER

Full Moon / Litha – Summer Solstice

The Full Moon is the height of the cycle that started with the New Moon. We want to experience life so much that we're bursting with it; we cannot contain the dynamic power that surges through us. The light of the Moon illuminates our lives, and the dreams that we've planted come to fruition. This is the phase that brings to life our visions and desires. It is also the time that illuminates any energies in our lives that are not harmonized. At the Full Moon, the Sun and Moon are opposing one another. Between the light of both luminaries, there is nowhere to hide. Our shadow is reflected back at us and we are forced to work with this tension if we don't want unintegrated archetypes

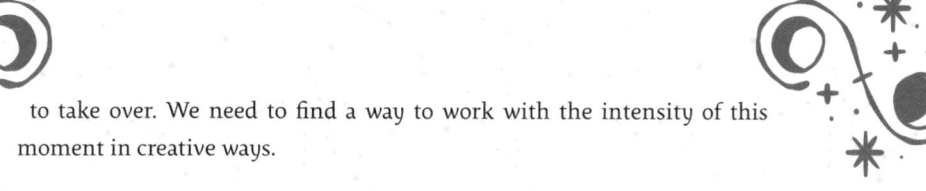

to take over. We need to find a way to work with the intensity of this moment in creative ways.

You can think of the Full Moon energy in the same way you think of the summer solstice, which is the height of the Sun's power. It's the crowning of the solar gods – while simultaneously marking the start of their descent. The longest day of the year shows off the power of the Sun, but it's also the moment when the Sun weakens, and days will begin to grow shorter. During this festival, nature is exploding with blossoms, with bountiful fruits and crops; the excess of life is manifesting all around us.

Waning Gibbous / Lammas

The time of Waning Gibbous, also called the Disseminating Moon, is a time of gratitude and giving back. We've witnessed and expressed our energy at the Full Moon, and now we're gathering all that we've grown and nurtured. It's a time to enjoy the fruits of our labor with friends and family. It's a time of gathering, sharing and communicating with our tribes and communities. This phase brings the most social time in a monthly cycle. The Disseminating Moon helps us connect with our people and share what we've learnt and gathered, be they material, emotional, intellectual or spiritual fruits. It's a time of merriment.

This chimes with the celebration of Lammas or Lughnasadh, when shortly after the euphoria of the height of summer we need to collect all the fruits of our yearly labor. This festival begins the seasons of harvest, and it's a celebration of our work – an expression of gratitude for the bountiful harvest and the beautiful crops that we can collect. After months of sowing seeds, planting our dreams, tending them, nurturing and protecting them, then watching them grow and blossom, we can finally reap the bounty and share it with our tribe.

SHEDDING THE LIGHT & AUTUMN

Third Quarter Moon / Mabon – Autumn Equinox

The Third Quarter Moon is another crisis point in the Moon cycle. At the First Quarter, we're asked to recommit to the dream and vision, in order to fulfil it. At the Third Quarter, we are asked to let go of that which is no longer required. It's a moment to review the cycle and the obstacles and blessings we've encountered, in order to learn the meaning behind them all. This phase helps us make difficult but necessary decisions and release or cut away all that is old, rotten and no longer contributes to our wellbeing; this is so we can make space for new ideas, new seeds, new growth.

To feel the energy of the Third Quarter Moon, think about the autumn equinox when the Sun reaches equilibrium and day equals night. From that moment on, the Sun is overtaken by darkness with every passing day. Nights are longer and days are shorter. It's the time of the Sun's yearly descent into the mythical underworld. Days grow colder; nature bursts in the last frenzied display of color before letting go of its beauty and bounty, shedding leaves in preparation for hibernation. After the harvest season ends, it's time to review our crops, and we must separate the chaff from the wheat. We must discern healthy fruits from those that begin to rot. This phase teaches us about discarding that which no longer serves us; that which will spoil the fruits of our labor if we allow it to be left unchecked. It's not a matter of obsessive purity, but a matter of survival.

Waning Crescent / Samhain – All Hallows' Eve

After the third quarter comes the Waning Crescent, or Balsamic phase. Those three days before the New Moon are a time of withdrawal. This time alone allows us to process and reflect on the past – past month, past year, past life... The end of the cycle is a time of deep, soulful reflection, without which we have no ability for conscious transformation. Like nature during late autumn, we must strip ourselves bare and retreat into our innermost place. Only then can we hope for a mystical communion with our own soul.

To best understand the Balsamic phase, we can reflect on the festival of Samhain, which begins when all the work of the harvest is done, and the world turns bare in preparation for winter. Leaves have fallen and the Earth has been washed clean by the winds and rain. At a time when people depended on nature and the turning of the seasons, this stage of the year was the most crucial in their fight for survival. The animals were brought in from the pasture, and the weakest ones that would not survive through winter were chosen to be slaughtered. Their sacrifice would hopefully sustain the community throughout the coldest months. Preparation for darkness and the harshness of winter made people nervous, as their very survival depended on the length of the winter and the food gathered and stored. Samhain, a fire festival which observed the thinning of the veil between this life and the next, was born from the inescapable awareness of mortality. The power of nature herself makes us search for answers; divination and communing with ancestors were part of the process. This is the most reflective part of the year, where we look back at where we came from and how much we've achieved, not only in the last year, but in the years gone, as a family, a tribe, a community. This is a time to acknowledge our roots and ancestry and reflect on the gifts and obligations that we were given by those who came before us.

CREATING YOUR MOON RITUAL

imply put, ritual is a meaningful activity that we practice at regular intervals, or in a special time of celebration. Having a cup of morning tea, eating birthday cake, putting up a Christmas tree or celebrating Shabbat or Diwali... All of these activities fall under the umbrella of "ritual." Rituals mark important transitions in our lives (like births, graduations etc.) and help us communicate that external change in life to our subconscious mind.

The main difference between this morning cup of tea and a tea ceremony is the purpose behind them. When we consciously set out to perform a set number of actions and steep them with meaning, we elevate everyday customs into an experience for our own souls. When we set an intention, we uplift the simple act of making tea into a ceremony that has significance and the potential for transformation.

Any rite performed in times or places of transition has the ability to help us connect with a part of us which exists beyond words, logic and rational understanding. It is the part of us that thinks in symbols and movement; it does not understand linear time because it, itself, is beyond time and communicates in hunches, in a voice of intuition, in insights, flashes of inspirations and dreams. Ritual is a bridge between our world and the inner realm of our own souls, between our actions and our hidden desires. It's a way to communicate with a part of us that is not easily accessible, allowing us to cross the threshold between the conscious and unconscious minds.

Here, I invite you to create your own ritual that you can perform at each New and Full Moon. This will help you develop a practice that you will follow every time you sit down with your journal. It will elevate the simple act of writing into a meaningful conversation with your soul and will change your mindset from mundane to sacred. By customizing your ritual for the New and Full Moon phase and working through those set steps before each journaling session, you are getting more sensitized to those specific energies, which in turn will help you become more aware of them in your everyday life.

Each of these private ceremonies can be tailored to each specific Moon phase by adding symbols of the particular zodiac sign that you are working with that month. Your practice can be deepened even further by gathering the elements that mean something to you or represent the Moon phase and the zodiac sign you're engaging with. This is because their symbolism speaks directly to that unconscious part of you that communicates through images and feelings, and in turn, helps you set intentions that are aligned with your soul, with that Moon phase and with the sign's archetypal energy.

How to create your own ritual:

These prompts will help you make your New and Full Moon journaling a special and sacred time of communicating and communing with your self, your soul, your inner world. Use this reminder every month to set up a space and create a rite with intention and meaningful repetition.

✦ Consider how big or small you want this ritual to be. It is not about elaborate theatrics but about something meaningful to you. It can be anything from a five-minute meditation with a candle to a whole evening of a cleansing bath, journaling and chanting.

✦ Consider how much time it will take, and when to do this ritual. You want to create a meaningful space for your self-care, and not add the pressure of squeezing intricate productions in between other commitments.

✦ Contemplate the intention for each ritual, as this will guide your decisions.

✦ Consider the tools that can help you get connected to the energy of the phase and add meaning to the rite. This could include candles, incense or essential oil, a favorite pen, or a bell or singing bowl to ring at the beginning of the session. Any tool that helps you enter a transformational space will do.

✦ Create a sacred space. It can be as small as a special scented candle that is only used for this occasion, or as elaborate as a private altar.

✦ Decide whether you'll change or add anything to your ritual depending on the element or the zodiac sign that you're working with that month.

✦ Tailor it monthly – look at the zodiac sign the Moon is in and choose symbols that represent this energy. If you have your birth chart, you can find which house the Moon is currently transiting through, and include symbols which reflect that house's themes.

A SAMPLE MOON RITUAL TO GET YOU INSPIRED

(Example based on New Moon in Taurus for Capricorn rising)

Moon phase: the New Moon in Taurus in my fifth house (my Ascendant is Capricorn, therefore Taurus falls into my fifth house)

Setting up my sacred space:
I spread the blanket that I use only for this work on the floor in front of the shelf with my altar space. I have my pen and my journal to hand. On my altar, I place a white candle, a bell and frankincense incense as I do for all my New and Full Moon ceremonies.

For Taurus, I have a beautiful orchid in a pot representing the Earth, beauty and speaking to my five senses (Taurus is an earth sign), and my notebook that represents *The Astro-Luna Journal* (the fifth house is one of creativity).

Ritual steps:

✦ I close my doors and make sure I will not be disturbed.

✦ I light the candle and incense, and I state my intention: "I plant seeds of practical creativity in my life."

✦ I ring the bell once to acknowledge that my sacred time has begun.

✦ I sit down on my blanket, close my eyes, take a few deep breaths and check in with my body: is it relaxed, is there a tension or discomfort somewhere? I adjust my posture accordingly.

✦ I sit in meditation for 10 minutes, breathing and looking at the flame of the candle and the beautiful orchid and the notebook. I allow my mind to focus on the symbols on the altar.

✦ I read through *The Astro-Luna Journal's* description of the Taurus New Moon

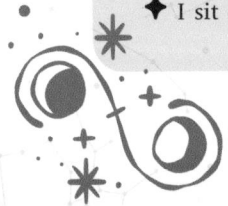

to help me connect and understand those energies better. (See: Vol 2, Your Astro-Luna Journal.) I also read about the symbolism of the fifth house. (See: Vol 3, Mansions in The Sky.)

✦ I am ready to take my journal and pen and write my intention for this New Moon: to use this energy to help me design something beautiful and practical at the same time.

✦ I write down the thoughts, feelings and reflections that came up during my meditation and my reading about the symbolism. I use journal prompts to go even deeper.

✦ When I finish, I close my eyes and take a few more deep breaths.

✦ I ring the bell three times to acknowledge the end of my ritual.

✦ I blow out the candle and incense and clear my space.

✦ I take the feeling and connection created with me into my everyday life.

YOUR RITUAL

This is the space for you to design your own ritual that you will follow at each New and Full Moon. You can consider the symbolism of the individual zodiac sign in the monthly section in the next chapter. Write down what tools you will need (candles, incense, mala etc.) and what actions (lighting a candle, chanting or saying a prayer) you will take at the beginning of each New or Full Moon ritual. Make this as simple or as detailed as you wish. Here you can design a transformational space for your journaling sessions.

NEW MOON RITUAL

New Moon keywords – new beginnings, new cycle, planting of ideas, fresh start, setting intention, introspection, reflection

_____
_____
_____
_____
_____
_____
_____
_____
_____
_____
_____
_____
_____
_____
_____
_____
_____
_____
_____
_____
_____
_____
_____
_____
_____
_____

FULL MOON RITUAL

Full Moon keywords – gratitude, celebration, release, fruition, blossoming, letting go, forgiveness, cleansing

VOL II

Welcome to the beating heart of this book.

Here you will get to know the elemental energies of the universe. You will be introduced to all 12 zodiac signs and become more familiar with their expressions. You will learn to recognize their energies, and way of working. In time, you will recognize their subtle influence in your life, too.

This volume is the cauldron of transformation. This is where your connections with the universe, with Luna and with your own soul will be forged. When used with intention and given the space this process requires, this journal can become your companion and guide you to both a deeper perception of the world around you and the whole universe of wonders within you.

THE 12 HEAVENLY ARCHETYPES

I f you're holding this journal, you might already be familiar with the zodiac wheel and the 12 signs from Aries to Pisces. Those 12 heavenly constellations were imagined by our ancestors as gods, goddesses and monsters, and given names and stories from Babylonian, Greek and other ancient mythologies. Each of them had their own energy and personality, and western astrology uses symbols of those 12 mythical archetypes to explain and translate the language of the stars. For example, Aquarius is the Water Bearer: he holds the celestial vessel containing the water of life. This sign can tell us a lot about what nourishes our unique spark. Libra, the Scales, can teach about mortal and divine justice, about a life lived in harmony and balance. We can expand our understanding of the cosmos by studying those individual signs, and by looking for connections between them. Each of them is associated with one of four **elements** – fire, water, earth, air – which means there are three archetypes per element. We also have four zodiac signs in each of the **modalities** (cardinal, fixed and mutable) and all 12 signs are equally divided between two **polarities** (active and passive).

Elements, modalities and polarities, explained in detail below, split the zodiac into different areas, giving us additional insight into each individual archetype, and showing us how they relate to one another. This understanding of connections between zodiac signs can be really helpful if we want to work on something specific (like this Moon phase journal) for a longer period of time.

Let's say you want to create something sustainable and practical, which is what the earth element is all about. You might want to check dates for all the New Moons in **earth element** signs (Taurus, Virgo and Capricorn) and make sure that for each of those New Moons you set up the same intention, you carry the same vision, and you use that time to really bring change in an earthy, material, practical way. Another example might be a new project that is bold, inspirational and pioneering. **Cardinal energy** can help with this, so you can find the cardinal signs of the zodiac (Aries, Cancer, Libra and Capricorn) and set your intention on the New Moon that falls in those signs, as they most resonate with that spearheading energy of your project.

The beauty of those fundamental blocks of our zodiac is that you can mix and match. Let's say you want to start building a house or a business that is strong, resilient and stable. You would look for the **element of earth** for the practical application of that energy, and to the **fixed modality** to ensure whatever is being built can be reliable for a long time. The sign that is both **earth** and **fixed** is Taurus, so the New Moon in Taurus might be a great beginning for this project, for setting up intents, for writing your goal in your journal and brainstorming practical steps to achieve it.

Our lives are not one dimensional – they are just the opposite. They are the spectrum of activity ranging from new jobs and new relationships, to the familiar stability of our home life, to the depth of our passions and spiritual life. The yearly cycle of the astrological luminaries brings focus and energy to each area of our lives. As we begin the journey with the New Moon in each of them, we begin to follow this subtle energy and get more sensitized to it. Below, you have more information about those prime divisions of the zodiac archetypes and the building blocks of universal energy.

ELEMENTS

Elements symbolize the main **quality** of energy. They form the four bricks from which our symbolic cosmos is built. They represent the nature of the world around us and our human psyche. With fire symbolizing inspiration, water our emotions, air our thoughts and earth our bodies, we can begin to view the world through those four forms and see how all of life is the interplay between them all.

Fire (Aries, Leo, Sagittarius)
Fire signs are those that show the fire of enthusiasm and passion, as well as a flair for the dramatic. They have a strong vision, and their courage and missions are intricately linked to their goals.

Earth (Taurus, Virgo, Capricorn)
Earth signs are grounded and reliable. They are the practical, loyal and solid ones of the zodiac. Their connectedness is through the Earth herself, and also through the body and the five senses.

Air (Gemini, Libra, Aquarius)

Air signs are the thinkers of the zodiac. They are full of ideas, data and information. They are networkers and communicators.

Water (Cancer, Scorpio, Pisces)

Water signs are the reservoirs of emotion, as well as familial past and ancestral memories. They are refreshing, charming and sensitive. They are overflowing with visions and dreams.

MODALITY

This classification talks about the energy **type**. How do we use the energy? To inspire and initiate (cardinal), to build and stabilize (fixed), or to change and let go (mutable)? Modality is calculated from each sign's position in relation to the four seasons, and each modal type can be linked with the symbolism of that time of year.

Cardinal (Aries, Cancer, Libra, Capricorn)

Cardinal signs are those that mark turning points and begin new seasons. In the Northern Hemisphere, Aries starts spring with the spring equinox; during Cancer season, we celebrate the summer solstice; Libra begins fall with the autumn equinox; Capricorn opens winter season with the winter solstice. Those signs have the cardinal energy of those seasons: they initiate and begin things.

Fixed (Taurus, Leo, Scorpio, Aquarius)

Fixed signs fall at the height of each season. Aquarius is the midst of winter; Taurus is the crux of spring bloom; Leo is the heat and heart of summer; Scorpio is the depth of fall. Their energy brings the quality of being at the heart and center of the season. They stabilize, persist and sustain. They are loyal, reliable and hold strong beliefs.

Mutable (Gemini, Virgo, Sagittarius, Pisces)

Mutable signs fall at the end of each season, when one energy is letting go before a new beginning. Pisces releases winter and washes away the frost; Gemini enjoys the energy of spring while getting us excited for summer;

Virgo ends the summer season with harvest to prepare for autumn; Sagittarius ponders the meaning of fall before the first frost of winter descends. Mutable signs are on the threshold: still firmly grounded in one season, but able to see the possibility of new things to come. They are unrestricted, adaptable, and versatile: they go with the flow of life, of information.

POLARITY

This classification talks about the current and **direction** of energy. We can liken astrological polarity to magnetic poles, or to the scientific approach in which positive consumes energy, and negative produces it. Polarity does not imply or assign the value of the energy. Positive does not mean "good" and negative does not mean "bad" – it just shows the direction the energy is flowing in. Another way to consider these two poles is as active versus receptive, with active energy being focused outward, while receptive is more internally reflective. Classically, these two distinctions are also known as masculine and feminine (see below for further exploration of this idea).

Positive/Active/Masculine

Active signs are fire and air signs (Aries, Gemini, Leo, Libra, Sagittarius, Aquarius). Their energy is directed outwards: it's extroverted, needing interaction. Active signs are stimulated by what surrounds them, as they are concerned and motivated by rewards and events in the outside world. They thrive when they are doing things, sparking change and collaborating with others.

Negative/Receptive/Feminine

Receptive signs are earth and water signs (Taurus, Cancer, Virgo, Scorpio, Capricorn, Pisces). Their energy is directed inward: it's introverted and needs reflection. Receptive signs are responsive by nature. They are subtle, concerned with the world of emotions and psychological stimuli. They thrive in solitude and are comfortable when self-contained. They are motivated by inner strength, talents and gifts.

ASTROLOGY AND GENDER

As you go through this journal you might encounter gender pronouns in descriptions of the Sun/Moon or zodiac signs. In the language of astrology, I use those pronouns to describe the energy flow – its polarity – and not to imply social gender. Pronouns help us differentiate between active and receptive energy.

Sadly, in our western, patriarchal society, we separate certain personality traits and emotions by gender, and in a very simplistic way assign qualities like aggression and competitiveness to men (Mars qualities), while traits such as affection and harmony are linked with women (Venus qualities). In fact, each planet that represents those attributes rules two signs – masculine/active sign in air or fire, and feminine/receptive sign in earth or water. Astrology teaches us that qualities of the planet Mars (like drive, aggression and lust) can be experienced in both the energetic functions of active/masculine Aries (linked with the archetype of athlete and warrior) as well as receptive/feminine Scorpio (linked with the archetype of psychotherapist or femme fatal).

Aggression is the same energy, regardless of whether it is expressed in the active, outgoing way of a warrior fighting an enemy, or in the receptive way of a psychotherapist fighting inner demons. Astrology shows us just that, revealing that there is no space for the apparently biological division of social gender, but there *is* for the function of the energy, which exists in each of us.

Personally, when I use this language, it is purely to reclaim the energetic and functional understanding of those archetypes and not to refer to a specific gender, because all of those possibilities are present in our horoscope, despite our gender identity. The beauty of our birth chart shows the spectrum of expressions of those archetypes and describes our unique soul path, which we then manifest through who we are in the world.

YOUR ASTRO-LUNA JOURNAL

ARIES

Aries, the first sign of the zodiac, is bold, boisterous and brave. This archetype rushes into new adventures headfirst without much thought, reacting instead to inner desires. Aries is the pioneer of the zodiac. As a cardinal fire sign, Aries is all about initiating actions, breaking new ground and boldly going where no one has gone before. They do not wait around or plan ahead, but instead plunge straight into action. Aries loves taking charge, starting new projects and following his own impulsiveness. People born under the sign of Aries value their freedom and need independence. This strong assertive energy can help establish and protect our boundaries. Misused, it can come out as competitiveness and quickly morph into conflict. Aries does not like to be challenged and this raw energy can turn violent, aggressive and destructive if not expressed in a healthy way.

INFO/ATTRIBUTES

- **Polarity:** Positive/active/masculine
- **Modality:** Cardinal
- **Element:** Fire

- **Planetary ruler:** Mars
- **Motto:** "I am."

KEYWORDS

- New beginnings
- Anger
- Freedom
- Competitiveness
- Instinct
- Initiative
- Desire
- Pioneer

- Independence
- Self-interest
- Individuality
- Daring
- Adventurous
- Impulsive
- Natural expression

NEW MOON IN ARIES

The New Moon in Aries can help us connect with the fire inside of us. It brings up that raw, initiating energy that we need to start taking steps that will bring us closer to the goals and visions we set over the Pisces season. This is the perfect time to take action to bring those dreams into fruition. The New Moon in Aries is good for any new beginnings, especially those that require courage and strength from us. Any endeavors that have pioneering elements can benefit from Aries energy. Use the time of the New Moon to set an intention to help you tap into your fearlessness, your tenacity and determination, your impulsive actions and your pure desire for freedom.

Record the details of this New Moon, including which house the Moon is transiting through in your birth chart (if you have it).

Date: Sign degree: House placement:

_____

_____

_____

Set an intention for this cycle and plant the seed of a vision, a dream or an idea that you want to develop in the days and weeks to come.

_____

_____

_____

_____

_____

_____

_____

_____

_____

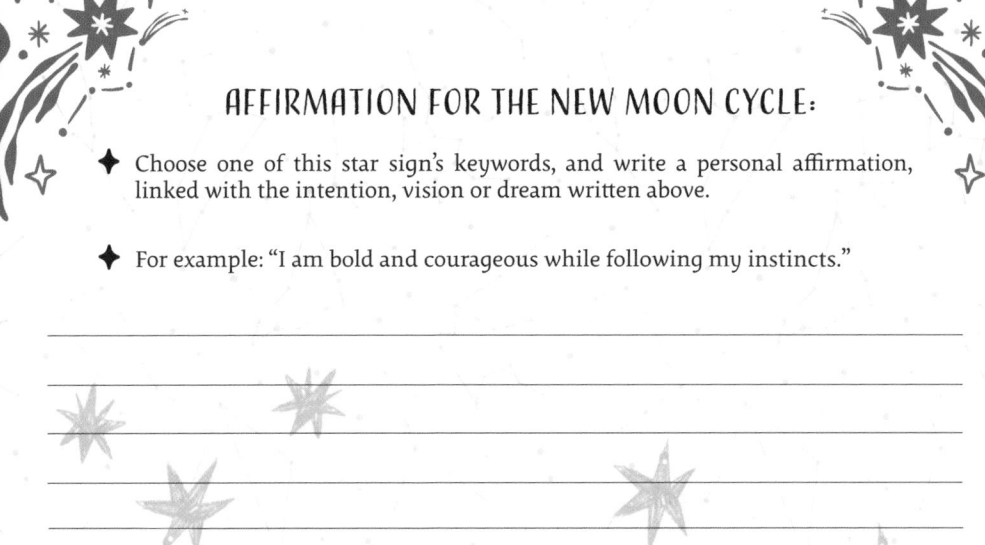

AFFIRMATION FOR THE NEW MOON CYCLE:

✦ Choose one of this star sign's keywords, and write a personal affirmation, linked with the intention, vision or dream written above.

✦ For example: "I am bold and courageous while following my instincts."

_____

_____

_____

_____

_____

JOURNAL PROMPTS AND SOUL QUESTIONS:

1. Reflection – Select one of the keywords; what does it mean to you? What emotions does it bring up? Choose the word that resonates most by attracting or repelling you. Journal on the meaning of that word. What does it represent to you, how do you see it manifested in the world around you, and how do you express it in your life? Plant your positive seeds at the New Moon and keep that keyword, your reaction to it and your affirmation, in mind during the coming cycle. This will help you to focus on the energy that you wish to manifest or embody in your life.

2. Aggression – How do you deal with anger and rage? Do you express them in an uncontrollable way, or do you keep them repressed? If you could express your anger in a healthy way, what would that look like? This cycle can help you examine this emotion and reflect on the roots of your behavior, so that you can make positive changes.

3. Courage – Where in your life can you make bold, courageous decisions or initiate action? Which areas of your life would benefit from you being more daring? What would you change or do, if you were not afraid? In this cycle, you might want to work with the energy of Aries to bring a bit more fire into your life and become the pioneer that you need to be.

JOURNAL ON THE NEW MOON

Note down your reflections on the archetype, thoughts from meditation, and answers to the journaling questions.

FULL MOON IN ARIES

The Full Moon in Aries shows us the fruits of all the new changes that we've dared to introduce in our lives. Luna highlights our internal courage and the natural expression that we have. It's a great time to be grateful for our freedoms and reflect on all those that do not enjoy the same privileges as we do, in whatever part of our life that might be. The Moon brings to light our courage to try new things, which we can be grateful for, but it also highlights all the areas where we've initiated action out of selfishness, impulsiveness or competitiveness. The Full Moon in Aries can bring tension between our own freedoms and compromises that we must make to honor our commitments.

Record the details of this Full Moon, including which house the Moon is transiting through in your birth chart (if you have it).

Date: **Sign degree:**   **House placement:**

_____

_____

_____

Write down what you are grateful for, what is blossoming in your life, or what you want to release and let go of at the height of this cycle.

_____

_____

_____

_____

_____

_____

_____

_____

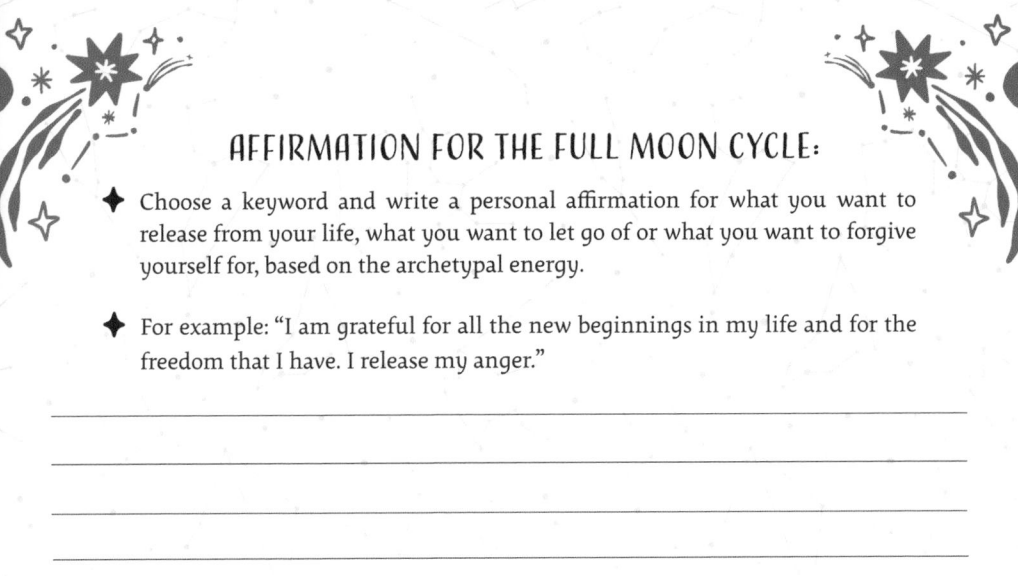

AFFIRMATION FOR THE FULL MOON CYCLE:

✦ Choose a keyword and write a personal affirmation for what you want to release from your life, what you want to let go of or what you want to forgive yourself for, based on the archetypal energy.

✦ For example: "I am grateful for all the new beginnings in my life and for the freedom that I have. I release my anger."

_____

_____

_____

_____

_____

_____

JOURNAL PROMPTS AND SOUL QUESTIONS:

1. Celebration and gratitude – Select one of the keywords and celebrate that feeling or trait in your life. Gratitude is a powerful emotion, helping us maintain our state of physical and emotional wellbeing. By practicing thankfulness on each Full Moon, you're getting into a rhythm of visualizing your dreams on the New Moon and expressing those dreams outwardly on the Full Moon. You can use the idea of celebration and gratitude as a journaling prompt: consider how your chosen keyword manifests in your life. Then, think about how you can celebrate this keyword more. Being aware of those blessings in your life will, in time, open your mind, so you can see even more things to be grateful for.

2. Independence – The Full Moon in Aries will shine a light on the tension between our need for independence and our commitment to others in our lives. Is your need for freedom your heart's true desire, or is it just an excuse to run away from responsibilities? How does your need for self-assertiveness affect your relationships?

3. Anger – This Full Moon can add energy that fuels our anger, so let's be mindful of the way we express it. Use the light of the Full Moon to give voice to strong negative emotions, as they too need to be disclosed. With the light of Luna, look for constructive ways of expressing your negative emotions and buried rage.

JOURNAL ON THE FULL MOON

Here's some space for you to write about all these themes, from practicing gratitude to shadow work.

_____
_____
_____
_____
_____
_____
_____
_____
_____
_____
_____
_____
_____
_____
_____
_____
_____
_____
_____
_____
_____
_____
_____
_____
_____

PREVIOUS NEW MOON IN ARIES

It can help to look back and reflect on where you were emotionally the last time there was a New Moon in Aries. This reflection can give you some perspective on where you are now. What has changed since then? Did you follow through on the intentions you set at that part of the cycle?

Date:　　　　　　　　**House placement:**

Reflection on the beginning of the cycle:

_____

_____

_____

_____

_____

_____

_____

_____

_____

_____

_____

_____

_____

_____

_____

_____

_____

_____

_____

_____

TAURUS

Resourceful and persistent, Taurus teaches us about the world through our senses. The wonder around us can be experienced through sight, touch, smell, taste and hearing – all of which are the body's responses or reactions to the stimuli of the world that surrounds us. It is through those functions that we experience beauty and pleasure. Taurus is also linked with the land, gardening and food. The bounty of Mother Nature sustains and nurtures our bodies and souls, not only through food but also through the sound of the birds and sea waves, through the fragrance of flowers and textures of the earth. We are connected with our world in a very literal sense, and when any of those connections are severed, we experience physical, emotional and psychological starvation.

When we begin to grasp this connection, we start to understand other attributes of Taurus like self-sufficiency, worth and possession. While this archetype is often linked to material worth, this sign informs our inner values – after all, we're spending our money on what we value. As a fixed earth sign, Taurus's main concern is sustaining stability, therefore the Bull is not quick to change. Taurus possesses nature's timing; change is inevitable, even if it is a slow process. It is unavoidable.

INFO/ATTRIBUTES

✦ **Polarity:** Negative/receptive/feminine

✦ **Modality:** Fixed

✦ **Element:** Earth

✦ **Planetary ruler:** Venus

✦ **Motto:** "I embody."

KEYWORDS

✦ Security
✦ Body
✦ Food
✦ Money

✦ Personal possessions
✦ Material attachments
✦ Five senses
✦ Perseverance

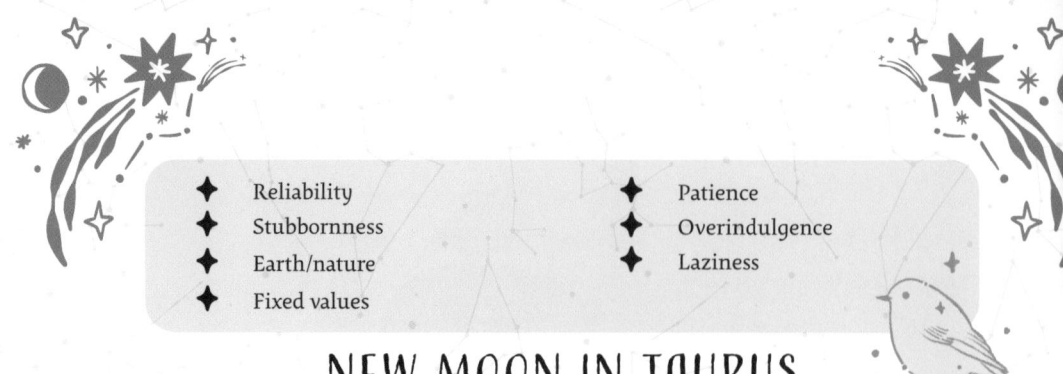

- Reliability
- Stubbornness
- Earth/nature
- Fixed values
- Patience
- Overindulgence
- Laziness

NEW MOON IN TAURUS

The New Moon in Taurus is a new beginning of a cycle around money and worth. It is a time of reviewing your finances and planning any changes for the future ahead. It is also a time to reflect on your inner values and priorities and consider whether they are aligned with your actions. You can use this New Moon's energy to make your environment safe, serene and a beautiful place to relax. You can also use this cycle to get in touch with your body and your senses through mindful eating, listening to the sounds of nature, going for a walk and experiencing the wind on your skin and feeding your eyes with new landscapes.

Record the details of this New Moon, including which house the Moon is transiting through in your birth chart (if you have it).

Date:　　　　　**Sign degree:**　　　　　**House placement:**

_____

_____

_____

Set an intention for this cycle and plant the seed of a vision, a dream or an idea that you want to develop in days and weeks to come.

_____

_____

_____

_____

_____

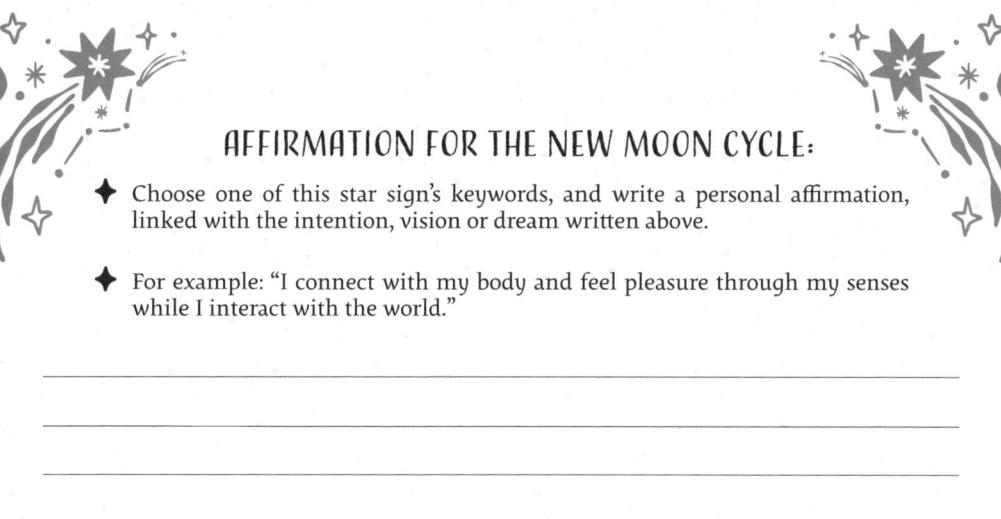

AFFIRMATION FOR THE NEW MOON CYCLE:

✦ Choose one of this star sign's keywords, and write a personal affirmation, linked with the intention, vision or dream written above.

✦ For example: "I connect with my body and feel pleasure through my senses while I interact with the world."

_____

_____

_____

_____

JOURNAL PROMPTS AND SOUL QUESTIONS:

1. Reflection – Select one of the keywords; what does it mean to you? What emotions does it bring up? Choose the word that resonates most by attracting or repelling you. Journal on the meaning of that word: what does it represent to you, how do you see it manifested in the world around you, and how do you express it in your life? Plant your positive seeds at the New Moon and keep that keyword, your reaction to it and your affirmation, in mind during the coming cycle. This will help you to focus on the energy that you wish to manifest or embody in your life.

2. Values –What is it that you spend your money on? Make a list of your core values, then make a list of the top ten things you spend money on after the essentials (e.g. food, gadgets, jewelry, nights out). Are those lists in sync? If they are not, what is the discrepancy? Why aren't you financially supporting your values, and is there anything that you pay for that goes against what you believe? Reflect on the differences and whether you can make an intention to bring them more in line with each other or to balance them.

3. Senses – How do you engage with and nourish your body and your senses? What is your relationship with them? Do you nurture them through beautiful music, nutritious food, by letting your eyes enjoy art or nature? Design a self-care ritual for one of the senses you think you might have neglected, and use the monthly cycle to nourish that part of you (e.g. spend an evening listening to soothing music or nature's sounds with your eyes closed to experience the world through your hearing).

JOURNAL ON THE NEW MOON

Note down your reflections on the archetype, thoughts from meditation, and answers to the journaling questions.

FULL MOON IN TAURUS

The Full Moon in Taurus is a celebration of your worth and your beauty, both external and internal. It is also a time of gratitude for the strength of your body. It's a time for appreciation of your sensuality and your connection to the Earth. It's a wonderful opportunity to treat yourself to something of value. The Taurus Full Moon can also shine a light on themes of self-worth and codependency in your life, and the struggles between feelings of security and vulnerability. At the time of the Full Moon in Taurus, use this energy to stay grounded.

Record the details of this Full Moon, including which house the Moon is transiting through in your birth chart (if you have it).

Date: **Sign degree:**   **House placement:**

_____

_____

_____

Write down what you are grateful for, what is blossoming in your life, or what you want to release and let go of at the height of this cycle.

_____

_____

_____

_____

_____

_____

_____

_____

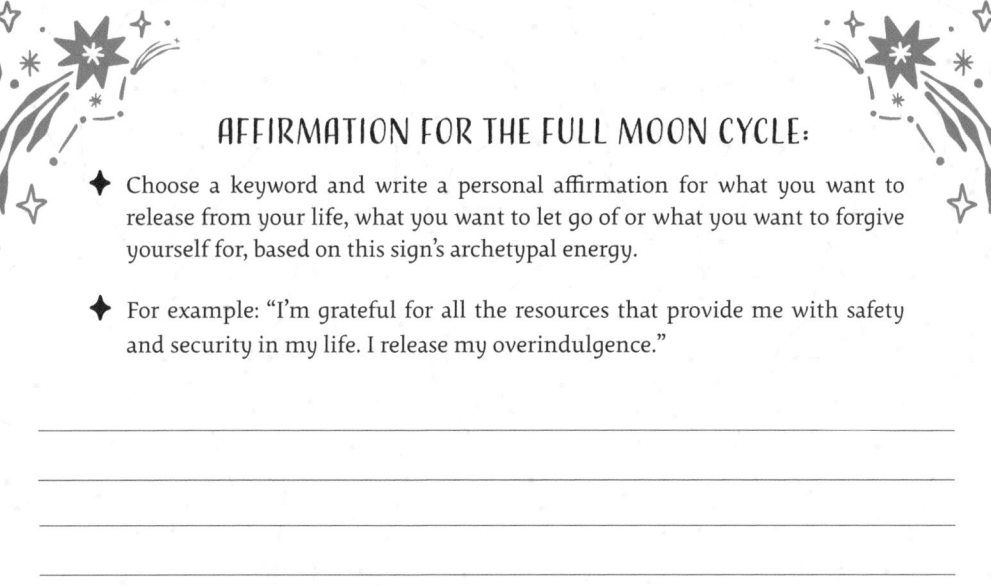

AFFIRMATION FOR THE FULL MOON CYCLE:

✦ Choose a keyword and write a personal affirmation for what you want to release from your life, what you want to let go of or what you want to forgive yourself for, based on this sign's archetypal energy.

✦ For example: "I'm grateful for all the resources that provide me with safety and security in my life. I release my overindulgence."

_____

_____

_____

_____

_____

JOURNAL PROMPTS AND SOUL QUESTIONS:

1. Celebration and gratitude – Select one of the keywords and celebrate that feeling or trait in your life. Gratitude is a powerful emotion, helping us maintain our state of physical and emotional wellbeing. By practicing thankfulness on each Full Moon, you're getting into a rhythm of visualizing your dreams on the New Moon and expressing those dreams outwardly on the Full Moon. You can use the idea of celebration and gratitude as a journaling prompt: consider how your chosen keyword manifests in your life. Then, think about how you can celebrate this keyword more. Being mindful and aware of those blessings in your life will, in time, open your mind, so you can see even more things to be grateful for.

2. Power – Acknowledge situations in life when you felt your own power. How did it align with your values and convictions? How can you bring more of this feeling into everyday life?

3. Growth – What in your life is growing and blossoming? Where in your life do you use your perseverance and stubbornness to create beauty? Celebrate whatever is flourishing, along with the strength that it took to achieve this growth.

JOURNAL ON THE FULL MOON

Here's some space for you to write about all these themes, from practicing gratitude to shadow work.

PREVIOUS NEW MOON IN TAURUS

It can help to look back and reflect on where you were emotionally the last time there was a New Moon in Taurus. This reflection can give you some perspective on where you are now. What has changed since then? Did you follow through on the intentions you set at that part of the cycle?

Date: **House placement:**

Reflection on the beginning of the cycle:

_____

_____

_____

_____

_____

_____

_____

_____

_____

_____

_____

_____

_____

_____

_____

_____

_____

_____

_____

♊ GEMINI ♊

Gemini, the twins of the zodiac, reminds us about the duality that exists within each of us. This is the duality of dark versus light, of bodily needs versus emotional needs, of being born in time and space versus being an immortal soul. This sign is teaching us about polarity and the idea that people, situations and objects have dark and light sides that are intrinsically connected. This archetype teaches us about diversity in the world, about new points of view or ways of life. We try to move through all that information looking for answers while creating more questions. Curiosity, humor, playfulness and charm are highlights of this sign. The twins are all about communicating in order to connect, and this mutable air sign will adjust to new ways of interaction and new environments easily.

INFO/ATTRIBUTES

- ✦ **Polarity:** Positive/active/masculine
- ✦ **Modality:** Mutable
- ✦ **Element:** Air

- ✦ **Planetary ruler:** Mercury
- ✦ **Motto:** "I think."

KEYWORDS

- ✦ Changeable
- ✦ Sociable
- ✦ Inquisitive
- ✦ Unreliable
- ✦ Messenger
- ✦ Storyteller
- ✦ Curious
- ✦ Intellectual inquisitiveness

- ✦ Speaking and writing
- ✦ Labeling
- ✦ Versatile
- ✦ Nosy
- ✦ Communicative
- ✦ Learning
- ✦ Connections

NEW MOON IN GEMINI

Gemini's New Moon is the beginning of a very social and fun cycle. This can be the start of a new network that you're connected with, new stories that you will hear and that you will share with others. This New Moon is an invitation to follow your curiosity and inquisitiveness to find more about the world around you, about the people around you, about things that you are already interested in. You might discover other things that you've never heard about before, which might become a new source of passion. This is a perfect cycle for being more sociable and connecting with others, but also for learning something new about the world, and about yourself. The New Moon in Gemini invites us not only to read and learn but also to write and share, so this might be the perfect month to start a journaling adventure.

Record the details of this New Moon, including which house the Moon is transiting through in your birth chart (if you have it).

Date: **Sign degree:**   **House placement:**

_____

_____

_____

Set an intention for this cycle and plant the seed of a vision, a dream or an idea that you want to develop in the days and weeks to come.

_____

_____

_____

_____

_____

_____

_____

_____

AFFIRMATION FOR THE NEW MOON CYCLE:

✦ Choose one of this star sign's keywords, and write a personal affirmation, linked with the intention, vision or dream written above.

✦ For example: "I appreciate my curiosity and ability to make new connections."

_____

_____

JOURNAL PROMPTS AND SOUL QUESTIONS:

1. Reflection – Select one of the keywords; what does it mean to you? What emotions does it bring up? Choose the word that resonates most by attracting or repelling you. Journal on the meaning of that word: what does it represent to you, how do you see it manifested in the world around you, and how do you express it in your life? Plant your positive seeds at the New Moon and keep that keyword, your reaction to it and your affirmation, in mind during the coming cycle. This will help you to focus on the energy that you wish to manifest or embody in your life.

2. Curiosity – Where is your curiosity? Do you nourish it by experiencing new things or is there a fear of the unknown within you? Maybe you have become complacent – comfortable with the knowledge that you have already accumulated. This cycle, I invite you to connect with your inner curiosity; start small and near. Get curious about your neighborhood: take a walk, explore new paths and pay attention to your surroundings. Exploring new routes can help you find something undiscovered and interesting in the place where you live. You can also get curious in your home: try out a new recipe or new entertainment. Notice and write in your journal how this journey of curiosity affects you.

3. Communication – This is a tough one as mindful communication is not often taught, and most of us listen to reply rather than listening to understand. I invite you to try an inner dialogue exercise this month. Try setting an intention to take a mindful pause when you're in conversation with someone, so that you can check in with yourself. Before replying, ask yourself what's really coming up emotionally, and where your response is coming from. Is it a place of understanding and compassion, a place of frustration, or a place of anger? Decide whether this is the right response for the situation. Your reply will be true to your inner values.

JOURNAL ON THE NEW MOON

Note down your reflections on the archetype, thoughts from meditation, and answers to the journaling questions.

FULL MOON IN GEMINI

At the time of the Full Moon in Gemini, we can express gratitude for all the lessons that we've learned, and for connections that are there to support us. The height of the cycle also shines a light on the ways we've communicated in the past. Have our words and stories been empowering, inspiring and moving, or have they all been superficial, disingenuous and misleading? At the height of Luna's cycle in Gemini, we are being asked to consider if we were communicating in order to connect with others. Were we communicating in authentic ways that created bridges between ourselves and others? Or were we communicating in order to bring other people down and spread false stories? During the peak of this cycle, we can also become more aware of the knowledge that we've been collecting in the past cycle. Did we collect it through a variety of sources, or are we stuck in our own echo chamber?

Record the details of this Full Moon, including which house the Moon is transiting through in your birth chart (if you have it).

Date: **Sign degree:**   **House placement:**

_____

_____

_____

Write down what you are grateful for, what is blossoming in your life, or what you want to release and let go of at the height of this cycle.

_____

_____

_____

_____

_____

_____

_____

_____

AFFIRMATION FOR THE FULL MOON CYCLE:

✦ Choose a keyword and write a personal affirmation for what you want to release from your life, what you want to let go of or what you want to forgive yourself for, based on the archetypal energy.

✦ For example: "I am grateful for my adaptable nature. I release my need for gossip."

_____

_____

_____

JOURNAL PROMPTS AND SOUL QUESTIONS:

1. Celebration and gratitude – Select one of the keywords and celebrate that feeling or trait in your life. Gratitude is a powerful emotion, helping us maintain our state of physical and emotional wellbeing. By practicing thankfulness on each Full Moon, you're getting into a rhythm of visualizing your dreams on the New Moon and expressing those dreams outwardly on the Full Moon. You can use the idea of celebration and gratitude as a journaling prompt: consider how your chosen keyword manifests in your life. Then, think about how you can celebrate this keyword more. Being mindful and aware of those blessings in your life will, in time, open your mind, so you can see even more things to be grateful for.

2. Communication – Using mindful awareness – and making sure you're not being judgmental towards yourself – reflect on how you have communicated over the past cycle. Be honest with yourself: did you share information or stories in a negative way, in a deceitful way, or in a way that spreads hurt? Write down what you can learn about yourself from those moments, and how you can let go of that behavior and forgive yourself for those mistakes.

3. Information – In the light of the Full Moon, you can see clearly what information is coming into your life and where it originates from. Do you have enough sources of varied (and sometimes conflicting) opinions to allow you to make your own informed decisions? Or is all the information coming from the same media outlet, social network or the same groups and societies? Are you in your own echo chamber that just feeds back what you already believe? Reflect on how you can expand your knowledge and understanding and widen your sources.

JOURNAL ON THE FULL MOON

Here's some space for you to write about all these themes, from practicing gratitude to shadow work.

PREVIOUS NEW MOON IN GEMINI

It can help to look back and reflect on where you were emotionally the last time there was a New Moon in Gemini. This reflection can give you some perspective on where you are now. What has changed since then? Did you follow through on the intentions you set at that part of the cycle?

Date: **House placement:**

Reflection on the beginning of the cycle:

CANCER

Cancer represents home, our roots and our family. It also speaks to our need for emotional and physical security. This is our innermost sanctuary which we protect and safeguard with ferocity. This archetype represents people that we care about and those who care about us – our own tribe. Cancer is also about conditioning: the way family, religion, culture and country can mold our thoughts and responses. Our roots and the way we were brought up are the foundation of everything we do in life. We either fight for family values or fight against them, but there is no denying that the family structure (or lack thereof) is a key ingredient of who we are as a person.

As a cardinal water sign, Cancer initiates the emotional processes that become the source of our behavior, our unconscious reactions to others and the hidden drives that push us forward or prevent us from going out in the world. Cancer energy holds those patterns that have been passed on to us by our family, our culture, our religion or nationality. It is the archetype of the foundation that makes us strong and grounded, as well as those structures of conditioning that hold us back. Our traditions and ancestral connections, like the waters of Cancer, should be a living embodiment of the love, gifts and nourishment that we've been given through generations; not fossilized structures that keep us so rigid that there is no flow in our lives.

INFO/ATTRIBUTES

+ **Polarity:** Negative/receptive/feminine

+ **Modality:** Cardinal

+ **Element:** Water

+ **Planetary ruler:** Moon

+ **Motto:** "I nurture."

KEYWORDS

+ Nurturing
+ Conditioning
+ Mothering
+ Comforting

+ Protective
+ Emphatic
+ Roots
+ Home

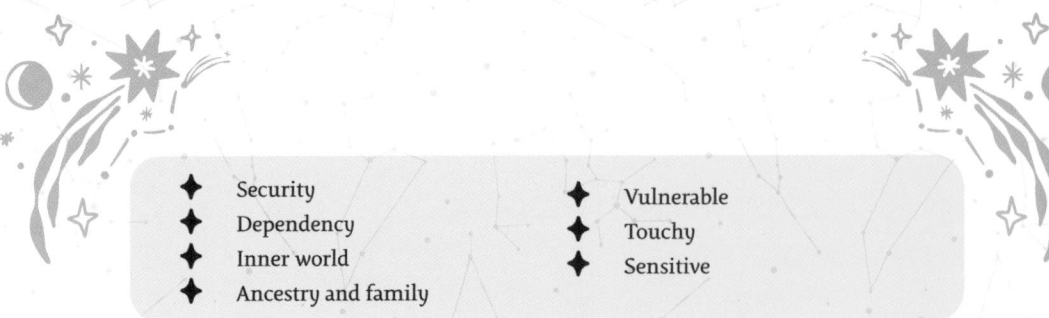

- ✦ Security
- ✦ Dependency
- ✦ Inner world
- ✦ Ancestry and family
- ✦ Vulnerable
- ✦ Touchy
- ✦ Sensitive

NEW MOON IN CANCER

The New Moon in Cancer invites us to go deep within our innermost sanctuary to rest, to take care of and nurture ourselves and to spend time with our family. This is a great cycle to spend with loved ones who make us feel safe, connected and understood. Cancer is a cardinal water sign that nourishes our vision and makes sure we have strong roots, so we are able to carry that into the world.

Record the details of this New Moon, including which house the Moon is transiting through in your birth chart (if you have it).

Date: **Sign degree:**   **House placement:**

_____

_____

_____

Set an intention for this cycle and plant the seed of a vision, a dream or an idea that you want to develop in the days and weeks to come.

_____

_____

_____

_____

_____

_____

_____

AFFIRMATION FOR THE NEW MOON CYCLE:

✦ Choose one of this star sign's keywords, and write a personal affirmation, linked with the intention, vision or dream written above.

✦ For example: "I feel connected to my family and my roots."

_____

_____

_____

JOURNAL PROMPTS AND SOUL QUESTIONS:

1. Reflection – Select one of the keywords; what does it mean to you? What emotions does it bring up? Choose the word that resonates most by attracting or repelling you. Journal on the meaning of that word: what does it represent to you, how do you see it manifested in the world around you, and how do you express it in your life? Plant your positive seeds at the New Moon and keep that keyword, your reaction to it and your affirmation, in mind during the coming cycle. This will help you to focus on the energy that you wish to manifest or embody in your life.

2. Tribe – Reflect on what family really means to you. Are you surrounded by your tribe? If you were lucky enough to be born into a loving and caring family, then how do you celebrate that? How do you show them you care? For a lot of us, our tribe are people we choose as our family for numerous reasons – how do we care for and nurture those relationships? Are you feeling nurtured and cared for? If not, what is it that you need to feel nurtured and how can you set an intention to receive that?

3. Nourishment – Reflect on nourishment in your life. How do you receive it from others and where in your life do you play the motherly figure yourself? Look within and review how you take care of your own emotional needs and where in your life you restrict your emotional expressions.

JOURNAL ON THE NEW MOON

Note down your reflections on the archetype, thoughts from meditation, and answers to the journaling questions.

FULL MOON IN CANCER

The energy of the Full Moon in Cancer brings light into our homes and all those places where we feel safe. If we are lucky enough to have comfort, security and nourishment for both our bodies and our souls, we can express gratitude. Luna's light also highlights the tension between the outside world of obligations and our inner world of family life. Do we hide at home to escape our calling or the hard work of mastering our craft? Reflect on your work/life balance. What does it mean to you?

Record the details of this Full Moon, including which house the Moon is transiting through in your birth chart (if you have it).

Date: **Sign degree:**   **House placement:**

_____

_____

_____

Write down what you are grateful for, what is blossoming in your life, or what you want to release and let go of at the height of this cycle.

_____

_____

_____

_____

_____

_____

_____

_____

_____

_____

_____

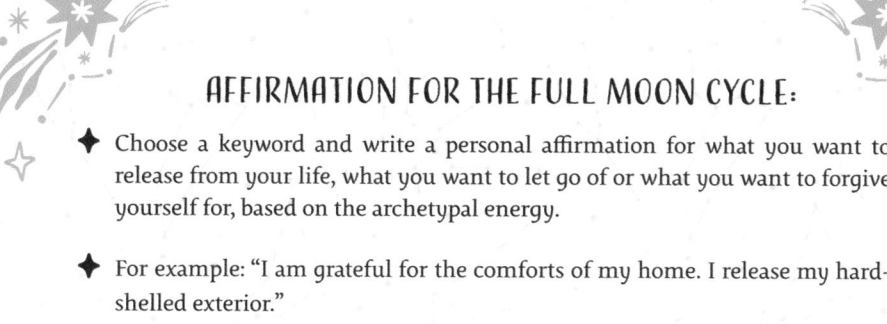

AFFIRMATION FOR THE FULL MOON CYCLE:

✦ Choose a keyword and write a personal affirmation for what you want to release from your life, what you want to let go of or what you want to forgive yourself for, based on the archetypal energy.

✦ For example: "I am grateful for the comforts of my home. I release my hard-shelled exterior."

_____

_____

_____

_____

JOURNAL PROMPTS AND SOUL QUESTIONS:

1. Celebration and gratitude – Select one of the keywords and celebrate that feeling or trait in your life. Gratitude is a powerful emotion, helping us maintain our state of physical and emotional wellbeing. By practicing thankfulness on each Full Moon, you're getting into a rhythm of visualizing your dreams on the New Moon and expressing those dreams outwardly on the Full Moon. You can use the idea of celebration and gratitude as a journaling prompt: consider how your chosen keyword manifests in your life. Then, think about how you can celebrate this keyword more. Being mindful and aware of those blessings in your life will, in time, open your mind, so you can see even more things to be grateful for.

2. Conditioning – What are some of the principles and judgments that you grew up with? Ask yourself: do they still hold true for you and how you are choosing to live your life? If not, then are they ultimate truths or just your family's values? Make a list of five of your family "truths" and make an intention to review them during the month.

3. Tradition – What does tradition and family mean to you? How are you relating to the environment you were brought up in, and what elements helped you create emotional stability and a solid foundation on which to stand strong to face the world?

JOURNAL ON THE FULL MOON

Here's some space for you to write about all these themes, from practicing gratitude to shadow work.

PREVIOUS NEW MOON IN CANCER

It can help to look back and reflect on where you were emotionally the last time there was a New Moon in Cancer. This reflection can give you some perspective on where you are now. What has changed since then? Did you follow through on the intentions you set at that part of the cycle?

Date: **House placement:**

Reflection on the beginning of the cycle:

_____

_____

_____

_____

_____

_____

_____

_____

_____

_____

_____

_____

_____

_____

_____

_____

_____

_____

LEO

Leo, ruled by the Sun, is where we shine! This is where we show off who we truly are, and like a child we see a world full of wonder as we recognize the uniqueness of our soul. We want to reveal who we are. We want to shine and be recognized (and applauded) for the exceptional person that we were born to be. We experience the pure joy that comes with a childlike quality. The fire of creativity burns bright in Leo, bringing pride, melodrama and self-centeredness. This is also the energy of generosity, joy and artistry.

Leo is a fixed fire sign and is all about maintaining and persevering in artistic pursuits and coming into one's creative power. It is also the true power of leadership coming from within. Expressing the desires of one's heart is a strong drive with this archetype. With Leo, we learn about the childlike joy in our hearts. We also recognize our courage and fearlessness in pursuit of happiness.

INFO/ATTRIBUTES

✦ **Polarity:** Positive/active/masculine

✦ **Modality:** Fixed

✦ **Element:** Fire

✦ **Planetary ruler:** Sun

✦ **Motto:** "I create."

KEYWORDS

✦ Inner child
✦ Creativity
✦ Leadership
✦ Courage
✦ Personal power
✦ Heart
✦ Bossy
✦ Drama

✦ Romance
✦ Approval
✦ Pride
✦ Vitality
✦ Generosity
✦ Enthusiasm
✦ Warmth

NEW MOON IN LEO

The New Moon in Leo is a wonderful time to get to know your inner child and use this cycle to bring more joy into your life. This world is full of wonder and beauty. If we were to see this world for the first time today, we would be in awe at the variety of species living on this planet; the intricate interconnectedness of the ecosystem itself; the creativity of people who, through millennia, created wonderful cultures and societies. When we reach adulthood, we are so conditioned to think in a certain way that we no longer look at the world with wonder. We seem to grow out of our ability to experience innocent joy. This month is a perfect opportunity to rediscover what makes our hearts truly full and happy. This is also a fantastic time to ask yourself this question: "If you were not afraid, what would you create?" Leo invites us to fall in love with the world again.

Record the details of this New Moon, including which house the Moon is transiting through in your birth chart (if you have it).

Date: **Sign degree:**   **House placement:**

_____

_____

Set an intention for this cycle and plant the seed of a vision, a dream or an idea that you want to develop in the days and weeks to come.

_____

_____

_____

_____

_____

_____

_____

_____

_____

_____

AFFIRMATION FOR THE NEW MOON CYCLE:

✦ Choose one of this star sign's keywords, and write a personal affirmation, linked with the intention, vision or dream written above.

✦ For example: "I create with courage and heart."

_____

_____

_____

JOURNAL PROMPTS AND SOUL QUESTIONS:

1. Reflection – Select one of the keywords; what does it mean to you? What emotions does it bring up? Choose the word that resonates most by attracting or repelling you. Journal on the meaning of that word: what does it represent to you, how do you see it manifested in the world around you, and how do you express it in your life? Plant your positive seeds at the New Moon and keep that keyword, your reaction to it and your affirmation, in mind during the coming cycle. This will help you to focus on the energy that you wish to manifest or embody in your life.

2. Creativity – What does creativity mean to you, and how important is it to your self-expression? Think about something that expresses your personality – your dress style, cooking, home decor, etc. Why did you choose to express yourself that way? Was it a conscious choice, or unconscious? Would you like to express yourself differently, and if so, what has been holding you back? Is there anything that gives you joy, but has long been buried under the mountain of responsibility?

3. Romance– Romantic comedies convinced us that Mr./Mrs./Mx. Right is what we need to feel whole. How can you create romance in your life just for yourself? Are you in love with your own self? This monthly cycle, take yourself out on a date to a place that you love. Go out and have a meal by yourself, go to the movies, or have a spa day. Remind yourself of how you want to be treated, how to be in love with yourself. If time is tricky, try to set aside an hour a week for a nice book and tea or to play a favorite video game. Treat yourself to something special – something that brings you joy.

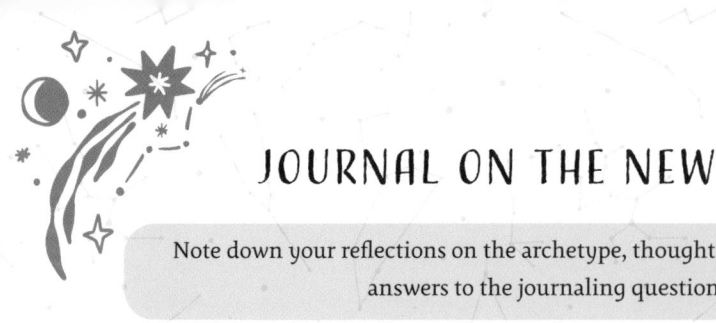

JOURNAL ON THE NEW MOON

Note down your reflections on the archetype, thoughts from meditation, and answers to the journaling questions.

FULL MOON IN LEO

When the light of Luna is shining in the sign of Leo, she brings heightened energy to a sign that already loves the spotlight. This can increase our need to be the center of attention and create drama around our own self-centered needs. A positive expression of this energy is the celebration of our heart's truest joy. In this, we can find the courage to live our truth and share our light with the world. However, this Full Moon can bring tension between that truth and the fear of not fitting in socially, of being rejected by our friends. This is the time to reach for that light within you and step into a leadership position, so you can be a shiny beacon of fearless expression.

Record the details of this Full Moon, including which house the Moon is transiting through in your birth chart (if you have it).

Date: **Sign degree:**   **House placement:**

_____

_____

_____

Write down what you are grateful for, what is blossoming in your life, or what you want to release and let go of at the height of this cycle.

_____

_____

_____

_____

_____

_____

_____

_____

_____

_____

AFFIRMATION FOR THE FULL MOON CYCLE:

✦ Choose a keyword and write a personal affirmation for what you want to release from your life, what you want to let go of or what you want to forgive yourself for, based on the archetypal energy.

✦ For example: "I am grateful for the joy in my life. I release the need for drama."

_____

_____

_____

JOURNAL PROMPTS AND SOUL QUESTIONS:

1. Celebration and gratitude – Select one of the keywords and celebrate that feeling or trait in your life. Gratitude is a powerful emotion, helping us maintain our state of physical and emotional wellbeing. By practicing thankfulness on each Full Moon, you're getting into a rhythm of visualizing your dreams on the New Moon and expressing those dreams outwardly on the Full Moon. You can use the idea of celebration and gratitude as a journaling prompt: consider how your chosen keyword manifests in your life. Then, think about how you can celebrate this keyword more. Being mindful and aware of those blessings in your life will, in time, open your mind, so you can see even more things to be grateful for.

2. Drama – How do you find drama in your life? Is it through good books, interesting movies and TV shows... or through workplace gossip and friends' life issues? We need attention and recognition but should ensure that we are asking for applause based on our own creative expression, and not by sharing drama that is not ours to share. Be honest with yourself: when was the last time you created some drama in your life? How do you feel about that now?

3. Fearlessness and courage – Like the lion from _The Wizard of Oz_, we sometimes search outside ourselves for qualities that we already possess. Instead of concentrating on what you don't have, write down a list of situations in which you felt or expressed courage. Maybe you stood up for someone in your group of friends whose life drama was providing material for gossip. Perhaps you said "hello" to a shopkeeper for the first time despite social anxiety gripping at your throat. Make a list of all big and small acts of courage and celebrate them. Challenge yourself to do more things that scare you and start with small steps.

JOURNAL ON THE FULL MOON

Here's some space for you to write about all these themes, from practicing gratitude to shadow work.

PREVIOUS NEW MOON IN LEO

It can help to look back and reflect on where you were emotionally the last time there was a New Moon in Leo. This reflection can give you some perspective on where you are now. What has changed since then? Did you follow through on the intentions you set at that part of the cycle?

Date: **House placement:**

Reflection on the beginning of the cycle:

_____

_____

_____

_____

_____

_____

_____

_____

_____

_____

_____

_____

_____

_____

_____

_____

_____

VIRGO

The sign of Virgo, as a mutable earth sign, shows us the paradox that we need change in order to gain stability. Earth is going through changes all the time, and yet it's the stability of her ecosystem that creates life. Life and astrology are full of paradoxes. Virgo teaches us about the need to review and adapt. We need to roll with all the changes that life brings, otherwise we are left unbalanced. This archetype shows us the ability to let go of what's holding us back in order to be fully present. As Baba Yaga instructed Vasilisa, we need to go through a laborious process of separating the chaff from the wheat, and there is no better season for it than Virgo season! When we live and work closely with the land, we learn discernment through harvest – we collect all the good, ripened produce and carefully separate them from anything that might be rotten, preventing the whole of our harvest from being spoiled.

Virgo helps us reflect on the past month, on our lives, and with a critical eye observe all the bountiful and beautiful fruits – which helps us let go of failure, anger, toxic thoughts and relationships. Letting go is not an option: it's compulsory if we want to maintain a healthy body and mind. One negative, persistent thought can spoil a great day. In Virgo, we learn what we should discard, so it does not hinder our lives. This sign reminds us to organize what we want to keep – and what we must release.

INFO/ATTRIBUTES

✦ **Polarity:** Negative/receptive/feminine

✦ **Modality:** Mutable

✦ **Element:** Earth

✦ **Planetary ruler:** Mercury

✦ **Motto:** "I analyze."

KEYWORDS

✦ Service
✦ Humility
✦ Discipline
✦ Critical thinking

✦ Discernment
✦ Healing
✦ Detail-oriented
✦ Organization

- Perfectionism
- Efficiency
- Modesty
- Self-doubt
- Skepticism
- Adaptability
- Analytical

NEW MOON IN VIRGO

The New Moon in Virgo invites us to look at our daily lives, our schedules, our patterns and our habits, and apply our mental faculties to discern whether they serve us in a healthy way. Does our daily routine help us maintain the wholeness of our bodies and our minds, or have we organized our lives in a way that causes unease through stress and anxiety? The new cycle in this sign invites us to look at our critical thinking and perfectionism and reflect on whether these traits are of service, or whether they are the weapons that we use to punish ourselves for not reaching unattainable perfection. This New Moon can bring healing if we can work with this energy and learn to see all those parts of our life, our thinking, our habits that no longer serve us and let them go.

Record the details of this New Moon, including which house the Moon is transiting through in your birth chart (if you have it).

Date:　　　　　　**Sign degree:**　　　　　　**House placement:**

_____

_____

Set an intention for this cycle and plant the seed of a vision, a dream or an idea that you want to develop in the days and weeks to come.

_____

_____

_____

_____

_____

AFFIRMATION FOR THE NEW MOON CYCLE:

✦ Choose one of this star sign's keywords, and write a personal affirmation, linked with the intention, vision or dream written above.

✦ For example: "I approach tasks with discipline and efficiency."

_____

_____

_____

JOURNAL PROMPTS AND SOUL QUESTIONS:

1. Reflection – Select one of the keywords; what does it mean to you? What emotions does it bring up? Choose the word that resonates most by attracting or repelling you. Journal on the meaning of that word: what does it represent to you, how do you see it manifested in the world around you, and how do you express it in your life? Plant your positive seeds at the New Moon and keep that keyword, your reaction to it and your affirmation, in mind during the coming cycle. This will help you to focus on the energy that you wish to manifest or embody in your life.

2. Purity – Virgo's purity does not mean sexual innocence or hygiene but rather, similar to science's use of the term to describe a substance, "pure" means free from contaminants, unmodified and whole. In Virgo, you can reflect and learn what it means to have that purity and be at one with your soul, body and mind, rejecting (to a certain degree) the contamination of societal pressure, social media, culture or family upbringing.

3. Service – After discovering your life and your light in Leo, now it's time to ask yourself: what lighthouse shines only for its own benefit? Virgo invites us to consider how we can shine our light for others. Journal on the ways you and your work can be of service to those around you.

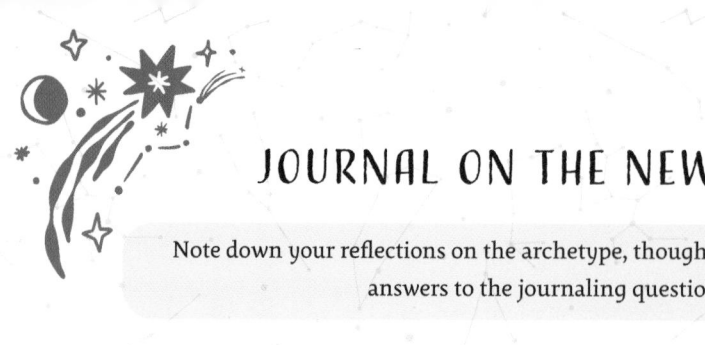

JOURNAL ON THE NEW MOON

Note down your reflections on the archetype, thoughts from meditation, and answers to the journaling questions.

_____
_____
_____
_____
_____
_____
_____
_____
_____
_____
_____
_____
_____
_____
_____
_____
_____
_____
_____
_____
_____
_____
_____
_____
_____
_____

FULL MOON IN VIRGO

The Full Moon in the sign of Virgo illuminates the daily routines that keep us grounded and contribute to our wellbeing, while also helping us be of service to others. This lunar cycle also heightens our critical thinking, self-doubt and perfectionism, so we need to be mindful not to get swept away with those energies, and avoid giving our inner critic too much power over us. This is the time to express gratitude for any part of your life that is whole and well, and to stay grounded in your routine to prevent yourself from being overwhelmed by repetitive, negative thoughts.

Record the details of this Full Moon, including which house the Moon is transiting through in your birth chart (if you have it).

Date: Sign degree: House placement:

_____

_____

_____

Write down what you are grateful for, what is blossoming in your life, or what you want to release and let go of at the height of this cycle.

_____

_____

_____

_____

_____

_____

_____

_____

_____

AFFIRMATION FOR THE FULL MOON CYCLE:

✦ Choose a keyword and write a personal affirmation for what you want to release from your life, what you want to let go of or what you want to forgive yourself for, based on the archetypal energy.

✦ For example: "I am grateful for my discerning mind. I release the need for perfection."

_____

_____

_____

_____

JOURNAL PROMPTS AND SOUL QUESTIONS:

1. Celebration and gratitude – Select one of the keywords and celebrate that feeling or trait in your life. Gratitude is a powerful emotion, helping us maintain our state of physical and emotional wellbeing. By practicing thankfulness on each Full Moon, you're getting into a rhythm of visualizing your dreams on the New Moon and expressing those dreams outwardly on the Full Moon. You can use the idea of celebration and gratitude as a journaling prompt: consider how your chosen keyword manifests in your life. Then, think about how you can celebrate this keyword more. Being mindful and aware of those blessings in your life will, in time, open your mind, so you can see even more things to be grateful for.

2. Inner Critic – How do you approach your inner critic and how much power does this voice have over you? At the height of the cycle of Virgo, you can use your discernment to help you heal. The inner critic is often there to help and protect us, so you can use a simple technique of conversation with this voice to rebut the negativity it would have you believe. You can also just simply thank your inner critic for the warning and say that you'll choose to do it on your own. Then, let go, and forgive yourself and the critic.

3. Service to others – At the height of the Virgo Moon cycle, when you can appreciate being able to help others, try to be honestly aware of whether helping others comes at the cost of your own physical or mental health. How can you bring balance into this area of your life, and release your need to be of service so that you don't sacrifice your own wellbeing?

JOURNAL ON THE FULL MOON

Here's some space for you to write about all these themes, from practicing gratitude to shadow work.

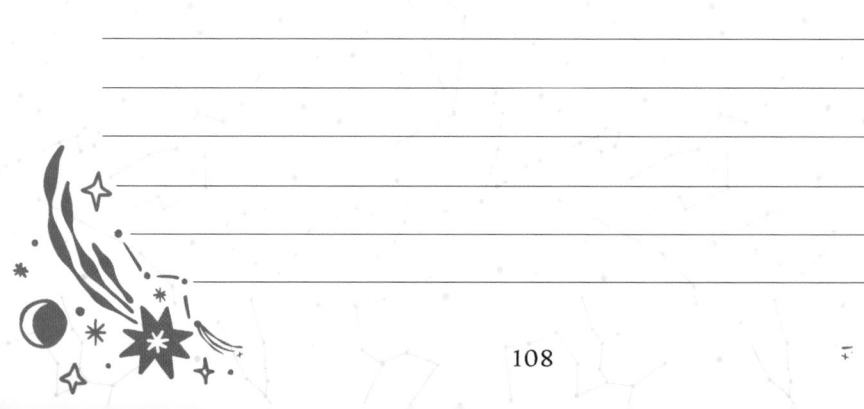

PREVIOUS NEW MOON IN VIRGO

It can help to look back and reflect on where you were emotionally the last time there was a New Moon in Virgo. This reflection can give you some perspective on where you are now. What has changed since then? Did you follow through on the intentions you set at that part of the cycle?

Date: **House placement:**

Reflection on the beginning of the cycle:

LIBRA

The Libra archetype helps us communicate with others in order to bring about balance and beauty. This cardinal air sign teaches us how to initiate new connections and gives us an opportunity to build harmonious relationships. With Libra, we are shown how to balance our own need for freedom and independence with companionship and belonging. To do so, we need to learn about being considerate, thoughtful and graceful. We need to develop a skilled use of diplomacy and mediation to resolve conflicts and misunderstandings that occur with close connections.

The energy of justice and fairness is dominant within Libra, and we are reminded that coexisting with others is a delicate balancing act. Relationships often reflect our internal world, and like a mirror, we can see our inner peace or struggle in those around us. Libra is also a sign linked with art, which can lift our spirits and communicate emotion, sometimes much better than any language would.

INFO/ATTRIBUTES

- **Polarity:** Positive/active/masculine
- **Modality:** Cardinal
- **Element:** Air

- **Planetary ruler:** Venus
- **Motto:** "I balance."

KEYWORDS

- Relationships
- Diplomacy
- Projection
- Aesthetic
- Art
- Charm
- Politeness

- Grace
- Idealism
- Social nature
- Consideration
- Harmony
- Balance
- Thoughtfulness

NEW MOON IN LIBRA

The new cycle in the sign of Libra invites us to examine the harmony within our relationships to discover whether there is a balance between our individual needs and those of others. As a cardinal air sign, Libra wants to initiate new connections, so during this cycle we might want to start new relationships or breathe fresh air into old ones. We might also want to further investigate any area of life that needs to be better balanced and set an intention to introduce more harmony. How is our inner world mirrored in the people around us? Can we see the connection? This is also a lovely time to express our thoughts using the language of the arts and connect with others through our creations.

Record the details of this New Moon, including which house the Moon is transiting through in your birth chart (if you have it).

Date: **Sign degree:**   **House placement:**

_____

_____

Set an intention for this cycle and plant the seed of a vision, a dream or an idea that you want to develop in the days and weeks to come.

_____

_____

_____

_____

_____

_____

_____

_____

_____

_____

AFFIRMATION FOR THE NEW MOON CYCLE:

✦ Choose one of this star sign's keywords, and write a personal affirmation, linked with the intention, vision or dream written above.

✦ For example: "I connect with beauty and harmony in my relationships."

_____

_____

_____

_____

_____

JOURNAL PROMPTS AND SOUL QUESTIONS:

1. Reflection – Select one of the keywords; what does it mean to you? What emotions does it bring up? Choose the word that resonates most by attracting or repelling you. Journal on the meaning of that word: what does it represent to you, how do you see it manifested in the world around you, and how do you express it in your life? Plant your positive seeds at the New Moon and keep that keyword, your reaction to it and your affirmation, in mind during the coming cycle. This will help you to focus on the energy that you wish to manifest or embody in your life.

2. Balance – Which area of your life feels out of balance at the moment? Can you use the Libran energy of the Moon to initiate new ways of communicating (with yourself as well as with others)? Libra means striving to find balance – however, to understand what is just and fair, we need to push boundaries and experience extremes on both ends of the spectrum.

3. Compromise – What is a good compromise for you? In a world that tells us there are only winners and losers, how can we communicate our needs and expectations to have them met efficiently? And how can we use clarity of mind to understand that when others' expectations oppose our own, there are other options and solutions rather than a fight? How do we find a balanced approach?

JOURNAL ON THE NEW MOON

Note down your reflections on the archetype, thoughts from meditation, and answers to the journaling questions.

FULL MOON IN LIBRA

This Full Moon's energy can fill us with joy for the harmony that we are experiencing in our lives. During this lunar cycle, take time to journal about your gratitude for those exquisite relationships that fill your life with grace, beauty and harmony. Luna will also bring to light tension in relationships where you have become so codependent that you are sacrificing your own harmony in order to sustain the connection. Pay attention to your inner struggles and those that you are experiencing with people around you. Let go of anything that is trying to tip your scales too far.

Record the details of this Full Moon, including which house the Moon is transiting through in your birth chart (if you have it).

Date: Sign degree: House placement:

_____

_____

_____

Write down what you are grateful for, what is blossoming in your life, or what you want to release and let go of at the height of this cycle.

_____

_____

_____

_____

_____

_____

_____

_____

AFFIRMATION FOR THE FULL MOON CYCLE:

✦ Choose a keyword and write a personal affirmation for what you want to release from your life, what you want to let go of or what you want to forgive yourself for, based on the archetypal energy.

✦ For example: "I am grateful for my diplomacy skills. I release the need to please everyone."

_____

_____

_____

_____

JOURNAL PROMPTS AND SOUL QUESTIONS:

1. Celebration and gratitude – Select one of the keywords and celebrate that feeling or trait in your life. Gratitude is a powerful emotion, helping us maintain our state of physical and emotional wellbeing. By practicing thankfulness on each Full Moon, you're getting into a rhythm of visualizing your dreams on the New Moon and expressing those dreams outwardly on the Full Moon. You can use the idea of celebration and gratitude as a journaling prompt: consider how your chosen keyword manifests in your life. Then, think about how you can celebrate this keyword more. Being mindful and aware of those blessings in your life will, in time, open your mind, so you can see even more things to be grateful for.

2. Beauty – Use the Full Moon energy to question any fake beauty standards that are having an influence on your life. Release your sense of obligation to beauty standards linked with your body, appearance, relationship and home that only highlight the outer shell, disregarding the inner life. In order to restore balance, you must let go of superficiality.

3. Toxic relationships – Bring awareness to any relationships that are based only on appearances. Because they are prioritizing superficial standards of external beauty, these relationships require you to sacrifice your own ideals and conform in order to keep them. Use this lunar cycle to learn when to let go of your need to be connected, because if that need supersedes your inner harmony, it will throw you out of balance.

JOURNAL ON THE FULL MOON

Here's some space for you to write about all these themes, from practicing gratitude to shadow work.

PREVIOUS NEW MOON IN LIBRA

It can help to look back and reflect on where you were emotionally the last time there was a New Moon in Libra. This reflection can give you some perspective on where you are now. What has changed since then? Did you follow through on the intentions you set at that part of the cycle?

Date: **House placement:**

Reflection on the beginning of the cycle:

_____

_____

_____

_____

_____

_____

_____

_____

_____

_____

_____

_____

_____

_____

_____

_____

_____

_____

_____

_____

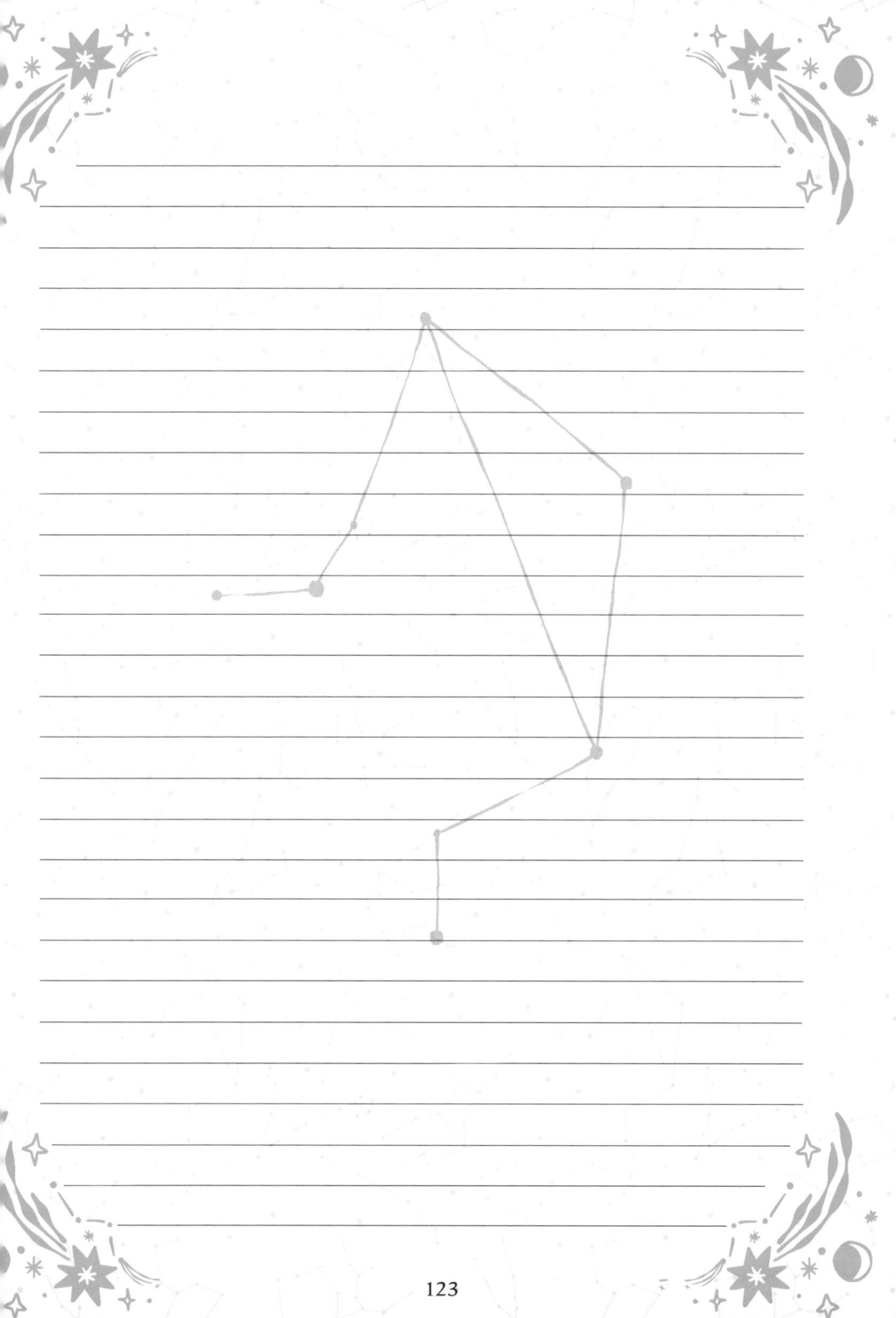

♏ SCORPIO

After meeting others in Libra and using communication to make connections, we encounter the realm of Scorpio. Our relationships are transformed and, in turn, become transformational as they intensify in emotion and intimacy. This is a space for deep healing and powerful regeneration. The connections we form in the Libran space of cooperation then lead to Scorpionic codependency. This can awaken potent feelings of either power or powerlessness, while giving us a need for control – which can lead to possessiveness.

Our intimate connections expose the places we are most vulnerable. We can use this deep honesty to reshape, regenerate and become stronger and more resilient – or we can recoil from this opportunity and become self-destructive, freezing in survival mode. Fear of this emotional depth can lead us to become so afraid that we hide behind masks of pride and power. Out of fear, we can sometimes manipulate people and situations to create a sense of stability. Scorpio at its best is power in vulnerability, raw honesty and depth of experience.

INFO/ATTRIBUTES

✦ **Polarity:** Negative/receptive/feminine

✦ **Modality:** Fixed

✦ **Element:** Water

✦ **Planetary ruler:** Mars (traditional), Pluto (modern)

✦ **Motto:** "I desire."

KEYWORDS

✦ Codependence
✦ Commitment
✦ Compulsion
✦ Obsession
✦ Transformation
✦ Survival
✦ Intuition
✦ Magnetism

✦ Mystery
✦ Charisma
✦ Intensity
✦ Intimacy
✦ Power
✦ Secrecy
✦ Manipulation

NEW MOON IN SCORPIO

The New Moon in Scorpio invites us to go deep into our emotions and strip back everything until we can see the naked truth of our inner world. This is the cycle that can help us explore our vulnerability and the depth of secrets. Luna's journey through Scorpio will teach us about the process of transformation, which is difficult and painful at times, but brings new life at its completion. The cycle of Scorpio reminds us that life and death are inseparable: for the new growth to sprout, a crack must open in the darkness of the Earth. This New Moon reflects on the depth of honesty in your life and your relationships. In what area of life are you called to transform?

Record the details of this New Moon, including which house the Moon is transiting through in your birth chart (if you have it).

Date: **Sign degree:**   **House placement:**

_____

_____

Set an intention for this cycle and plant the seed of a vision, a dream or an idea that you want to develop in the days and weeks to come.

_____

_____

_____

_____

_____

_____

_____

_____

AFFIRMATION FOR THE NEW MOON CYCLE:

✦ Choose one of this star sign's keywords, and write a personal affirmation, linked with the intention, vision or dream written above.

✦ For example: "I invite transformation and intensity into my life."

_____

_____

_____

_____

JOURNAL PROMPTS AND SOUL QUESTIONS:

1. Reflection – Select one of the keywords; what does it mean to you? What emotions does it bring up? Choose the word that resonates most by attracting or repelling you. Journal on the meaning of that word: what does it represent to you, how do you see it manifested in the world around you, and how do you express it in your life? Plant your positive seeds at the New Moon and keep that keyword, your reaction to it and your affirmation, in mind during the coming cycle. This will help you to focus on the energy that you wish to manifest or embody in your life.

2. Transformation/regeneration – In which area of life would you benefit most from regeneration? What does it mean to you? Transformation always entices us with the promise of something new and beautiful emerging, and we often forget that for new life to emerge, we need to go through the painful process of rebirth. Scorpionic transformation will lay us bare, if we allow ourselves to trust the process and step into the deep waters of Scorpio. Crisis and renewal can be cyclical. Power and powerlessness depend on our approach – do we take control of the narrative and allow the process to strip away another layer to transform into something new, or do we fight and struggle against it, potentially harming the outcome?

3. Power/powerlessness – How and where do you give your power away? What situation or people make you feel powerless? What resources (material, intellectual, spiritual, emotional) do you need to gather to feel more empowered? Can you remember a situation that made you feel like you had power? Can you reintegrate elements of that situation into your life now?

JOURNAL ON THE NEW MOON

Note down your reflections on the archetype, thoughts from meditation, and answers to the journaling questions.

_____
_____
_____
_____
_____
_____
_____
_____
_____
_____
_____
_____
_____
_____
_____
_____
_____
_____
_____
_____
_____
_____
_____
_____
_____
_____

FULL MOON IN SCORPIO

The Full Moon in Scorpio can bring a wonderful energy of gratitude for the constant metamorphosis of life, along with the strength and courage that we exhibited while going through this process. It also highlights the depth of intimacy that we have with others. The light of Luna shines into places that we would prefer to keep hidden, and reveals our secrets, our shadow and our obsessions. The intensity of this lunation can also trigger the tension between power and powerlessness in our lives, so stay fixed in your core emotional needs and don't let the waves of irrational energy sweep you off your feet.

Record the details of this New Moon, including which house the Moon is transiting through in your birth chart (if you have it).

Date: Sign degree: House placement:

_____

_____

_____

Write down what you are grateful for, what is blossoming in your life, or what you want to release and let go of at the height of this cycle.

_____

_____

_____

_____

_____

_____

_____

_____

_____

AFFIRMATION FOR THE FULL MOON CYCLE:

✦ Choose a keyword and write a personal affirmation for what you want to release from your life, what you want to let go of or what you want to forgive yourself for, based on the archetypal energy.

✦ For example: "I am grateful for my intuition and the power of my raw emotions. I release my obsessions."

_____

_____

_____

_____

JOURNAL PROMPTS AND SOUL QUESTIONS:

1. Celebration and gratitude – Select one of the keywords and celebrate that feeling or trait in your life. Gratitude is a powerful emotion, helping us maintain our state of physical and emotional wellbeing. By practicing thankfulness on each Full Moon, you're getting into a rhythm of visualizing your dreams on the New Moon and expressing those dreams outwardly on the Full Moon. You can use the idea of celebration and gratitude as a journaling prompt: consider how your chosen keyword manifests in your life. Then, think about how you can celebrate this keyword more. Being mindful and aware of those blessings in your life will, in time, open your mind, so you can see even more things to be grateful for.

2. Manipulation – Where in your life do you hold power over others (whether at home with your partner or children, at work or with your friends)? With the honesty of the Full Moon, can you judge whether that natural power dynamic has turned into manipulation? Is there any relationship in which you feel you are being manipulated, or where you feel someone is holding power over you?

3. Shadow – What secrets and obsessions do you hide from the world? Why do you spend your energy trying to keep these parts of yourself hidden away from prying eyes? What kind of power do they have over you? Would releasing those secrets and applying radical honesty help you regain your power and control?

JOURNAL ON THE FULL MOON

Here's some space for you to write about all these themes, from practicing gratitude to shadow work.

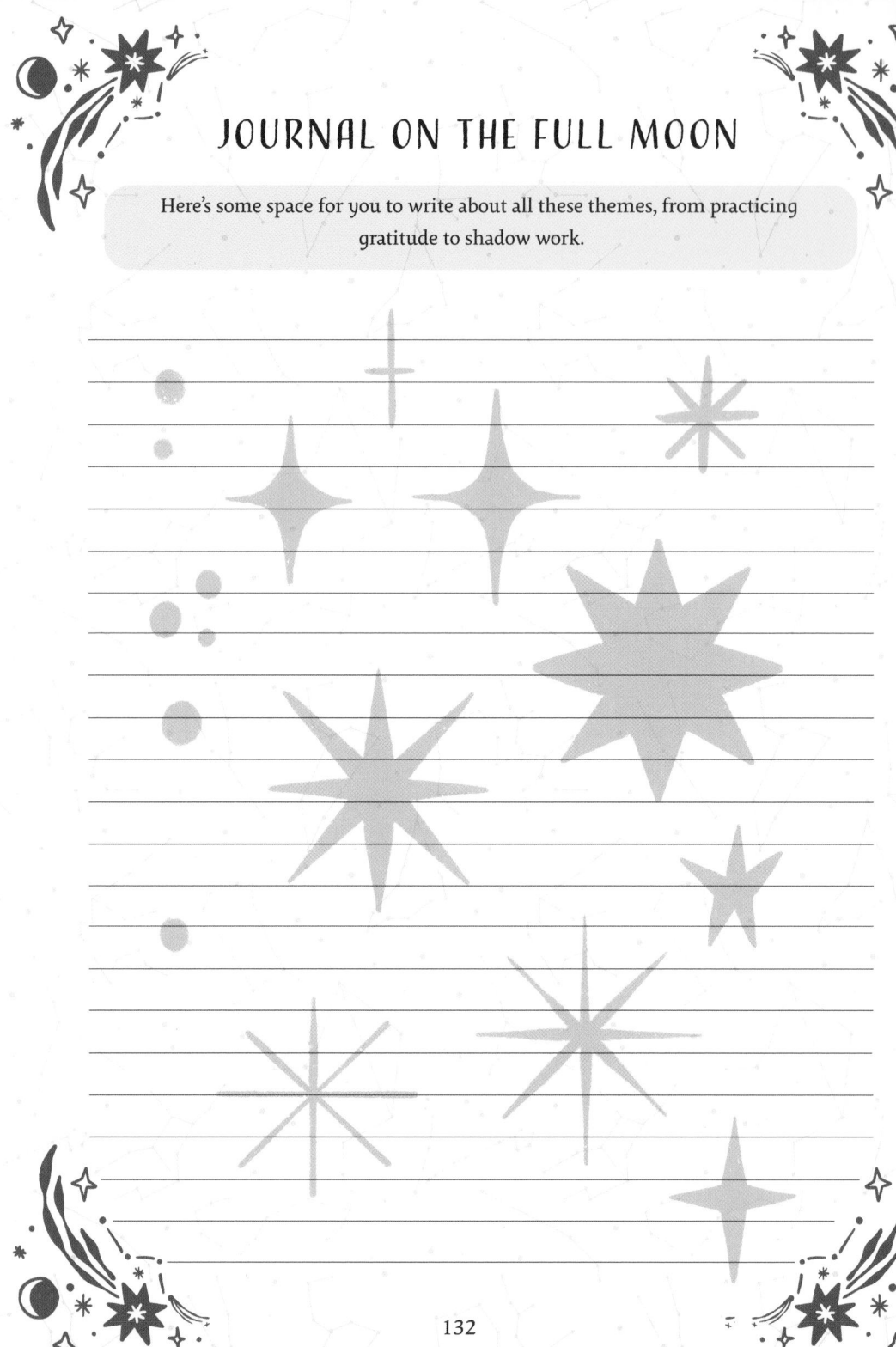

PREVIOUS NEW MOON
IN SCORPIO

It can help to look back and reflect on where you were emotionally the last time there was a New Moon in Scorpio. This reflection can give you some perspective on where you are now. What has changed since then? Did you follow through on the intentions you set at that part of the cycle?

Date: **House placement:**

Reflection on the beginning of the cycle:

_____

_____

_____

_____

_____

_____

_____

_____

_____

_____

_____

_____

_____

_____

_____

_____

_____

_____

SAGITTARIUS

When we emerge from the Scorpionic waters of metamorphosis, we see the light of a new day and we are inspired by the Sagittarian vision of the future. This archetype is the teacher of the zodiac. In Gemini, we collect data, we communicate and create a network; in Sagittarius, we put all those pieces of data together to see a bigger picture. Sagittarius gives us a sense of distance, so we can see our connections as a woven network of interconnectedness.

Sagittarius is a mutable fire sign, and his function is to spread philosophies and beliefs. He lights a fire of passion in us and helps us aspire to something bigger than we think we are. Sagittarius helps us listen to our intuition, as it tells us about the vast possibilities of life – and this inspires us to aim higher.

INFO/ATTRIBUTES

+ **Polarity:** Positive/active/masculine

+ **Modality:** Mutable

+ **Element:** Fire

+ **Planetary ruler:** Jupiter

+ **Motto:** "I discover."

KEYWORDS

+ Possibility
+ Faith
+ Teacher
+ Further education
+ Long-distance travel
+ Foreign
+ Meaning

+ Wisdom
+ Optimism
+ Expansion
+ Law
+ Wild nature
+ Great outdoors
+ Exploration

NEW MOON IN SAGITTARIUS

The New Moon in Sagittarius invites us on an adventure into the great outdoors, while opening the door to further education. Both physical and philosophical adventures can help us discover new possibilities and spread the fire of our own vision. This cycle promotes the exploration of different cultures, foreign lands, new philosophies and religious beliefs. It is a wonderful time to examine our faith and worldview. Anything that expands our awareness can benefit us during this time.

Record the details of this New Moon, including which house the Moon is transiting through in your birth chart (if you have it).

Date: Sign degree: House placement:

_____

_____

Set an intention for this cycle and plant the seed of a vision, a dream or an idea that you want to develop in the days and weeks to come:

_____

_____

_____

_____

_____

_____

_____

_____

_____

_____

AFFIRMATION FOR THE NEW MOON CYCLE:

✦ Choose one of this star sign's keywords, and write a personal affirmation, linked with the intention, vision or dream written above

✦ For example: "I am free to explore foreign lands, cultures and beliefs."

_____

_____

_____

JOURNAL PROMPTS AND SOUL QUESTIONS:

1. Reflection – Select one of the keywords; what does it mean to you? What emotions does it bring up? Choose the word that resonates most by attracting or repelling you. Journal on the meaning of that word: what does it represent to you, how do you see it manifested in the world around you, and how do you express it in your life? Plant your positive seeds at the New Moon and keep that keyword, your reaction to it and your affirmation, in mind during the coming cycle. This will help you to focus on the energy that you wish to manifest or embody in your life.

2. Adventure – Where in your life are you adventurous, or where would you like to be? Are you inclined to read and learn new things? What new culture or location would you like to discover, if you could go anywhere? What does adventure mean to you, and what possibilities does it open?

3. Meaning – Where in your life do you turn for meaning? Is it the religion of your ancestors, a new spiritual exploration, your intellect or your scientific approach? What philosophy or religion supports your decision-making? Does a specific belief system guide you in life? If you think of the judgements that you have made over the years, where did your concept of good and bad come from? Has that changed for you as you expanded your views by encountering foreign cultures and viewpoints?

JOURNAL ON THE NEW MOON

Note down your reflections on the archetype, thoughts from meditation, and answers to the journaling questions.

FULL MOON IN SAGITTARIUS

The Full Moon in Sagittarius highlights the wisdom and the freedom of expression that we can be grateful for. At this time, we can get excited about our dreams for the future, or the adventures we're about to embark on. This cycle also reveals any tension or opposition between what we've been told and foreign perspectives that we encounter – and this revelation challenges us to question what we believe and why we believe it. The Full Moon in Sagittarius illuminates the core values from which we profess judgement, and highlights any rigidity that has set in, as this does not allow for more exploration and discovery.

Record the details of this Full Moon, including which house the Moon is transiting through in your birth chart (if you have it).

Date: Sign degree: House placement:

_____

_____

_____

Write down what you are grateful for, what is blossoming in your life, or what you want to release and let go of at the height of this cycle.

_____

_____

_____

_____

_____

_____

_____

_____

_____

_____

AFFIRMATION FOR THE FULL MOON CYCLE:

✦ Choose a keyword and write a personal affirmation for what you want to release from your life, what you want to let go of or what you want to forgive yourself for, based on the archetypal energy.

✦ For example: "I am grateful for my teachers and their wisdom. I release fundamentalist and restrictive beliefs that I hold."

_____

_____

_____

JOURNAL PROMPTS AND SOUL QUESTIONS:

1. Celebration and gratitude – Select one of the keywords and celebrate that feeling or trait in your life. Gratitude is a powerful emotion, helping us maintain our state of physical and emotional wellbeing. By practicing thankfulness on each Full Moon, you're getting into a rhythm of visualizing your dreams on the New Moon and expressing those dreams outwardly on the Full Moon. You can use the idea of celebration and gratitude as a journaling prompt: consider how your chosen keyword manifests in your life. Then, think about how you can celebrate this keyword more. Being mindful and aware of those blessings in your life will, in time, open your mind, so you can see even more things to be grateful for.

2. Philosophy – What philosophy guides your judgement? Write down your five core beliefs. Where do they come from (e.g. religion, tradition, family values, cultural beliefs etc.)? Are they strong and unshakable because they are rooted in compassion? Or are they rigid, not allowing for exploration of opposing viewpoints? Have you ever been so convinced of your own truth that you closed off a part of yourself?

3. Teachers – Write down all the people in your life, whether scientific, intellectual or spiritual, that you look up to. In the piercing light of the Full Moon, examine any flaws, rigidity of judgement, or lack of common sense, and try to see them for who they are – flawed humans and not all-knowing oracles. How does this perspective change your attitude towards to them?

JOURNAL ON THE FULL MOON

Here's some space for you to write about all these themes, from practicing gratitude to shadow work.

PREVIOUS NEW MOON
IN SAGITTARIUS

It can help to look back and reflect on where you were emotionally the last time there was a New Moon in Sagittarius. This reflection can give you some perspective on where you are now. What has changed since then? Did you follow through on the intentions you set at that part of the cycle?

Date: **House placement:**

Reflection on the beginning of the cycle:

_____

_____

_____

_____

_____

_____

_____

_____

_____

_____

_____

_____

_____

_____

_____

♑ CAPRICORN ♑

Capricorn, as a cardinal earth sign, brings us the energy needed to develop a practical application of our Sagittarian dream. It's in Capricorn that we ask ourselves how to achieve what we've dreamed of. This sign expects discipline and commitment to our vision. Thanks to the earth element that grounds it, we can be very practical about setting up goals, step-by-step processes and deadlines to make those fiery aspirations a reality. Capricorn is like the coach that pushes us past our limits, forces us to commit, and encourages practice to achieve mastery, so that we can reach our goals. It brings maturity and a sense of responsibility to every project.

In this sign, we encounter authority. Here we ask ourselves if we can conform to societal norms, or if we clash with law and the establishment. Capricorn also teaches us about our own boundaries and internal authority. When we master a subject, whether it's meditation, cooking or quantum physics, we become an expert in that field and gain credibility based on the knowledge we built through hard work. This sign challenges us to build our own support structures.

INFO/ATTRIBUTES

✦ **Polarity:** Negative/receptive/feminine

✦ **Modality:** Cardinal

✦ **Element:** Earth

✦ **Planetary ruler:** Saturn

✦ **Motto:** "I master."

KEYWORDS

✦ Authority
✦ Mastery
✦ Structure
✦ Society
✦ Reality
✦ Repression
✦ Parental figure
✦ Accomplishment

✦ Tradition
✦ Discipline
✦ Maturity
✦ Boundaries
✦ Man-made law
✦ Commitment
✦ Responsibility

NEW MOON IN CAPRICORN

The New Moon in Capricorn starts a cycle in which we can explore our commitments. What does it mean to have a framework in life and where does yours come from? Did you build your structure on the traditions of your ancestors, family or culture? Or did you create a framework out of your own hard work and commitment, or because you chose to out of a sense of responsibility? This is the cycle when we can explore the meaning of authority, both in a personal sense as well as in the form of employers, governmental structures or religious jurisdictions. We can also begin new commitments and master a subject that we'd love to become an expert in.

Record the details of this New Moon, including which house the Moon is transiting through in your birth chart (if you have it).

Date: Sign degree: House placement:

_____

_____

Set an intention for this cycle and plant the seed of a vision, a dream or an idea that you want to develop in the days and weeks to come.

_____

_____

_____

_____

_____

_____

_____

_____

_____

_____

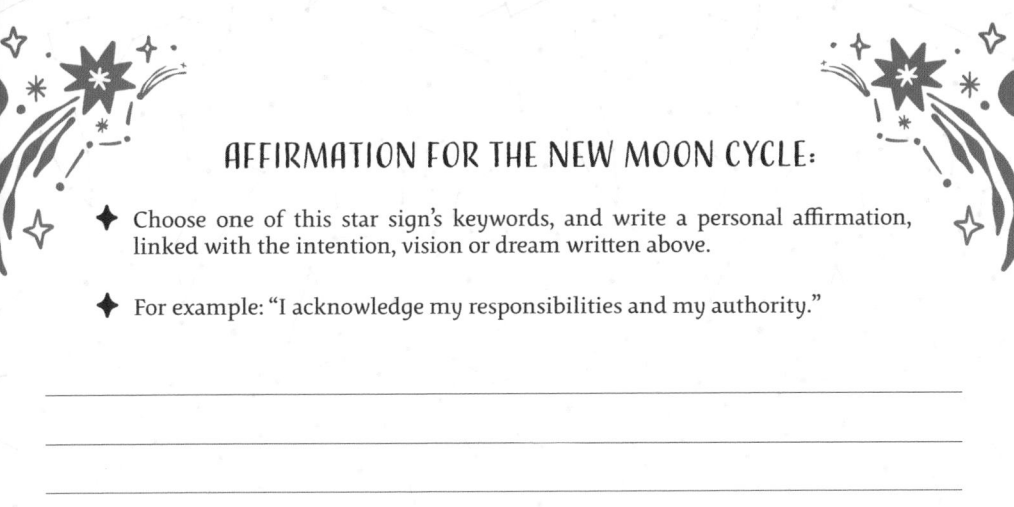

AFFIRMATION FOR THE NEW MOON CYCLE:

✦ Choose one of this star sign's keywords, and write a personal affirmation, linked with the intention, vision or dream written above.

✦ For example: "I acknowledge my responsibilities and my authority."

_____

_____

_____

_____

JOURNAL PROMPTS AND SOUL QUESTIONS:

1. Reflection – Select one of the keywords; what does it mean to you? What emotions does it bring up? Choose the word that resonates most by attracting or repelling you. Journal on the meaning of that word: what does it represent to you, how do you see it manifested in the world around you, and how do you express it in your life? Plant your positive seeds at the New Moon and keep that keyword, your reaction to it and your affirmation, in mind during the coming cycle. This will help you to focus on the energy that you wish to manifest or embody in your life.

2. Mastery and commitment – Where in your life would you like to achieve mastery? How can you create a structure to support yourself as you strive to achieve your goal? Is anything preventing you from committing to the task at hand? How do you hold yourself accountable for your own actions, your achievements and your failures?

3. Responsibilities – Reflect on the top five commitments in your life. Which of your responsibilities come from a deep sense of loyalty and dedication, and which originate in internalized societal expectations? How can we untangle those and work creatively so our commitment can be transformed into real devotion?

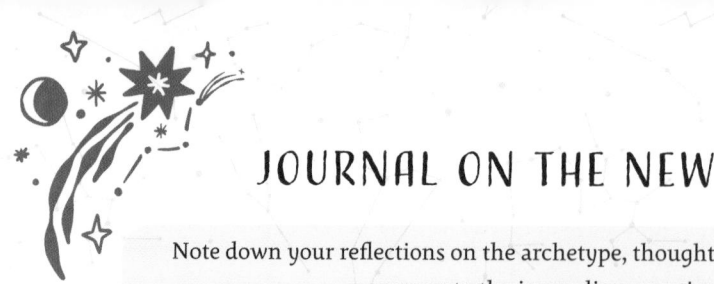

JOURNAL ON THE NEW MOON

Note down your reflections on the archetype, thoughts from meditation, and answers to the journaling questions.

_____
_____
_____
_____
_____
_____
_____
_____
_____
_____
_____
_____
_____
_____
_____
_____
_____
_____
_____
_____
_____
_____
_____
_____

FULL MOON IN CAPRICORN

The Full Moon in Capricorn highlights what we have achieved in life thanks to our hard work and determination. Giving thanks and recognizing our strength, commitment and perseverance in accomplishing those successes can be part of our Full Moon celebration. As always, Luna's light also reveals the tensions within the archetype, and asks whether in pursuit of mastery we have become too rigid, too strict, too hard on ourselves. Have we forgotten to nourish our emotional wellbeing?

Record the details of this Full Moon, including which house the Moon is transiting through in your birth chart (if you have it).

Date: Sign degree: House placement:

_____

_____

_____

Write down what you are grateful for, what is blossoming in your life, or what you want to release and let go of at the height of this cycle.

_____

_____

_____

_____

_____

_____

_____

_____

_____

AFFIRMATION FOR THE FULL MOON CYCLE:

✦ Choose a keyword and write a personal affirmation for what you want to release from your life, what you want to let go of or what you want to forgive yourself for, based on the archetypal energy.

✦ For example: "I am grateful for the support structures in my life. I release commitments that restrict me instead of supporting me."

_____

_____

_____

_____

JOURNAL PROMPTS AND SOUL QUESTIONS:

1. Celebration and gratitude – Select one of the keywords and celebrate that feeling or trait in your life. Gratitude is a powerful emotion, helping us maintain our state of physical and emotional wellbeing. By practicing thankfulness on each Full Moon, you're getting into a rhythm of visualizing your dreams on the New Moon and expressing those dreams outwardly on the Full Moon. You can use the idea of celebration and gratitude as a journaling prompt: consider how your chosen keyword manifests in your life. Then, think about how you can celebrate this keyword more. Being mindful and aware of those blessings in your life will, in time, open your mind, so you can see even more things to be grateful for.

2. Rigidity – Do you take yourself too seriously? Does anyone you know push you to be accountable? Where in your life do you encounter rigidity? What fuels you to meet your commitments and obligations? How do you nourish yourself and practice self-care? Or do you see self-care as a waste of time that could be better spent in more "productive" ways? How can you find a balanced approach?

3. Commitment versus family – Do your commitments affect your family life? Do any of your pursuits take up so much time and dedication that your home life is affected? Which of your obligations is secretly an escape from family commitments? Have you ever avoided spending time with family because you need to finish a project? Reflect on the subtle difference between dedication to your craft and using that as an excuse for not fulfilling other agreements.

JOURNAL ON THE FULL MOON

Here's some space for you to write about all these themes, from practicing gratitude to shadow work.

PREVIOUS NEW MOON
IN CAPRICORN

It can help to look back and reflect on where you were emotionally the last time there was a New Moon in Capricorn. This reflection can give you some perspective on where you are now. What has changed since then? Did you follow through on the intentions you set at that part of the cycle?

Date: **House placement:**

Reflection on the beginning of the cycle:

_____

_____

_____

_____

_____

_____

_____

_____

_____

_____

_____

_____

_____

_____

_____

_____

AQUARIUS

Aquarius is very much the rule breaker of the zodiac! This Water Bearer learnt from the previous archetype of Capricorn that rules, laws and regulations have their place only if they are in service of communities as a whole. Aquarius will not hesitate to challenge old paradigms if they no longer support humanity. Aquarius is an egalitarian, so this sign will fight for equal rights and advocate for changing regulations so that they serve a bigger community. In the negative expression, this energy might be used to break the rules just for the sake of breaking the rules, which is not a productive use of this archetype.

This fixed air sign has really strong ideas and is not easily swayed from his chosen course of action. On the opposite side of the zodiac, we have Leo, who invites us to create in order to garner appreciation; in Aquarius, we utilize that Leonian creativity in service of groups, neighborhoods and society. Aquarius innovates to make life easier for others, but according to his own vision. With his detached emotions, he can be the leader of a revolution and connect with like-minded people to create meaningful change.

INFO/ATTRIBUTES

- ✦ **Polarity:** Positive/active/masculine
- ✦ **Modality:** Fixed
- ✦ **Element:** Air
- ✦ **Planetary ruler:** Saturn (traditional), Uranus (modern)
- ✦ **Motto:** "I revolutionize."

KEYWORDS

- ✦ Intellect
- ✦ Eccentricity
- ✦ Originality
- ✦ Free thought
- ✦ Rebellion
- ✦ Reform
- ✦ Revolution
- ✦ Individual
- ✦ Independent
- ✦ Humanitarian
- ✦ Alienation
- ✦ Black sheep
- ✦ Tribe
- ✦ Detachment

NEW MOON IN AQUARIUS

The New Moon in Aquarius can bring a cycle of intellectual creativity and inspired innovations. This can be a great time to use out-of-the-box thinking to break any commitments in your life that are bogging you down, so that you can build something new. This is the cycle to revolutionize something within your life – but remember to use that spark of rebellion in service of the community. Like Prometheus, you can bring light and inspiration to your tribe. This is also a beautiful time to explore your own sense of uniqueness and maybe alienation, and to look for people around you who resonate with the same vibe. Maybe they can become your future tribe?

Aquarius' sense of loneliness comes from the insight that he has into the future and inner workings of society. He is on the outside looking in, which allows him to see structures that the rest of society might not be aware of yet. This is an isolated position. The power of this archetype comes from that insight – from spreading the message, attracting others to our cause and, in return, transforming structures to better support the tribe that we build around the ideas and ideals that we broadcast.

Record the details of this New Moon, including which house the Moon is transiting through in your birth chart (if you have it).

Date: Sign degree: House placement:

_____

_____

Set an intention for this cycle and plant the seed of a vision, a dream or an idea that you want to develop in the days and weeks to come.

_____

_____

_____

_____

_____

AFFIRMATION FOR THE NEW MOON CYCLE:

✦ Choose one of this star sign's keywords, and write a personal affirmation, linked with the intention, vision or dream written above.

✦ For example: "I appreciate my unique light and my independence."

_____

_____

_____

_____

JOURNAL PROMPTS AND SOUL QUESTIONS:

1. Reflection – Select one of the keywords; what does it mean to you? What emotions does it bring up? Choose the word that resonates most by attracting or repelling you. Journal on the meaning of that word: what does it represent to you, how do you see it manifested in the world around you, and how do you express it in your life? Plant your positive seeds at the New Moon and keep that keyword, your reaction to it and your affirmation, in mind during the coming cycle. This will help you to focus on the energy that you wish to manifest or embody in your life.

2. Uniqueness – Where in your life do you feel a sense of being misunderstood, or of alienation from others? How can you use this cycle to look for people who resonate with the same vibration, who are on the same wavelength as you? Which groups, societies, associations and organizations do you want to belong to, and what steps can you take during this cycle to feel part of your chosen tribe?

3. Gifts – Reflect on your special gifts and how you can use those talents in service of humanity. This may not have to be climbing a BP oil platform as an eco-activist, but it might be as simple as using your networking skills to bring local moms together, so they don't feel isolated at home with their children. We all have something special that we can offer to our community and this is the cycle for you to explore what it is that you can do.

JOURNAL ON THE NEW MOON

Note down your reflections on the archetype, thoughts from meditation, and answers to the journaling questions.

FULL MOON IN AQUARIUS

The Full Moon in Aquarius can bring an energy of celebration within your community. We can express gratitude for breaking through the restrictions that were limiting us in the past and celebrate our successes together. During this lunar cycle, be mindful that the energy of the Full Moon can also illuminate the shadow of this archetype. This can manifest as rebellion without a cause, and without any thought to what repercussions the community might suffer as a result. This can also manifest as a cold detachment, forgetting the opposing sign of Leo and the virtue of leading from the heart. If we fall prey to this shadow, we can get so wrapped up in our plans that we do not put our heart into them.

Record the details of this Full Moon, including which house the Moon is transiting through in your birth chart (if you have it).

Date: **Sign degree:**   **House placement:**

Write down what you are grateful for, what is blossoming in your life, or what you want to release and let go of at the height of this cycle.

AFFIRMATION FOR THE FULL MOON CYCLE:

✦ Choose a keyword and write a personal affirmation for what you want to release from your life, what you want to let go of or what you want to forgive yourself for, based on the archetypal energy.

✦ For example: "I am grateful for like-minded people. I release feelings of alienation."

_____

_____

_____

_____

JOURNAL PROMPTS AND SOUL QUESTIONS:

1. Celebration and gratitude – Select one of the keywords and celebrate that feeling or trait in your life. Gratitude is a powerful emotion, helping us maintain our state of physical and emotional wellbeing. By practicing thankfulness on each Full Moon, you're getting into a rhythm of visualizing your dreams on the New Moon and expressing those dreams outwardly on the Full Moon. You can use the idea of celebration and gratitude as a journaling prompt: consider how your chosen keyword manifests in your life. Then, think about how you can celebrate this keyword more. Being mindful and aware of those blessings in your life will, in time, open your mind, so you can see even more things to be grateful for.

2. Rebellion – Do you fight to deconstruct old structures, but without a clear plan of how to build something from their ashes? Who or what in your life brings up a strong need for rebellion? What is it about those structures, groups or boundaries that you feel so strongly about, and can you use the Full Moon in Aquarius to imagine a new reality?

3. Black sheep – What does this concept mean to you? Are you the black sheep or do you know someone who is cast in this role? Reflect on the function of the black sheep in the family and society at large. Why are they alienated? What is it about their uniqueness that the family unit or the culture cannot absorb? Can you think of any inspirational leaders – that you know personally or otherwise – who were considered black sheep?

JOURNAL ON THE FULL MOON

Here's some space for you to write about all these themes, from practicing gratitude to shadow work.

PREVIOUS NEW MOON
IN AQUARIUS

It can help to look back and reflect on where you were emotionally the last time there was a New Moon in Aquarius. This reflection can give you some perspective on where you are now. What has changed since then? Did you follow through on the intentions you set at that part of the cycle?

Date: **House placement:**

Reflection on the beginning of the cycle:

_____

_____

_____

_____

_____

_____

_____

_____

_____

_____

_____

_____

_____

_____

_____

_____

_____

♓ PISCES ♓

Pisces is the last of the zodiac archetypes and her power lies in adapting to the ebb and flow of life. Like fish in the sea, she senses the changing tides and adopts new directions. As a mutable water sign, Pisces also has the capacity to create change through her dreams. So many mystics, artists, activists and scientists started with a dream and ended up changing reality. Piscean sensitivity helps this sign get in tune with the zeitgeist; she can dive into the water of the unconscious and come back with a vision of a brave new world.

Being such a receptive and emphatic sign, the Piscean archetype is like a sponge, absorbing everything from her environment. This can leave her drained and exhausted. Good boundaries are not her strongest suit, so from time to time, she withdraws from society to be alone. This can take the shape of a meditation retreat, solo outdoor adventure, or staying at home to work on a piece of art or music. This zodiac sign can teach us the difference between being alone and being lonely. Spending time in solitude with the correct intention can deepen our relationship with life and with our dreams, and help us explore interconnectedness.

INFO/ATTRIBUTES

✦ **Polarity:** Negative/receptive/feminine

✦ **Modality:** Mutable

✦ **Element:** Water

✦ **Planetary ruler:** Jupiter (traditional), Neptune (modern)

✦ **Motto:** "I dream."

KEYWORDS

✦ Medium
✦ Hermit
✦ Addiction
✦ Escape
✦ Lack of boundaries
✦ Isolation
✦ Melancholy
✦ Compassion

✦ Sensitivity
✦ Suffering
✦ Lost of identity
✦ Victimhood
✦ Music
✦ Deception
✦ Dreams

NEW MOON IN PISCES

The New Moon cycle in Pisces brings us a time of dreams and healing. This is a gentle energy that invites us to dive into our visions and explore our dreams. Everything in the world that we have, from the clothes that we wear to the planes that we fly, used to be someone's dream before it was put into action and became reality. Take time during this cycle to be with yourself so you can pay attention to the gentle nudges of intuition. Diving into your inner world can bring rejuvenation and healing. In a world that glorifies hard work and burnout, the Pisces archetype has a lot of negativity attached to it. This cycle is for you to surrender to your inner world and your needs, and through music, poetry or art, reconnect with the collective mind.

Record the details of this New Moon, including which house the Moon is transiting through in your birth chart (if you have it).

Date: **Sign degree:**   **House placement:**

_____

_____

Set an intention for this cycle and plant the seed of a vision, a dream or an idea that you want to develop in the days and weeks to come.

_____

_____

_____

_____

_____

_____

_____

_____

_____

_____

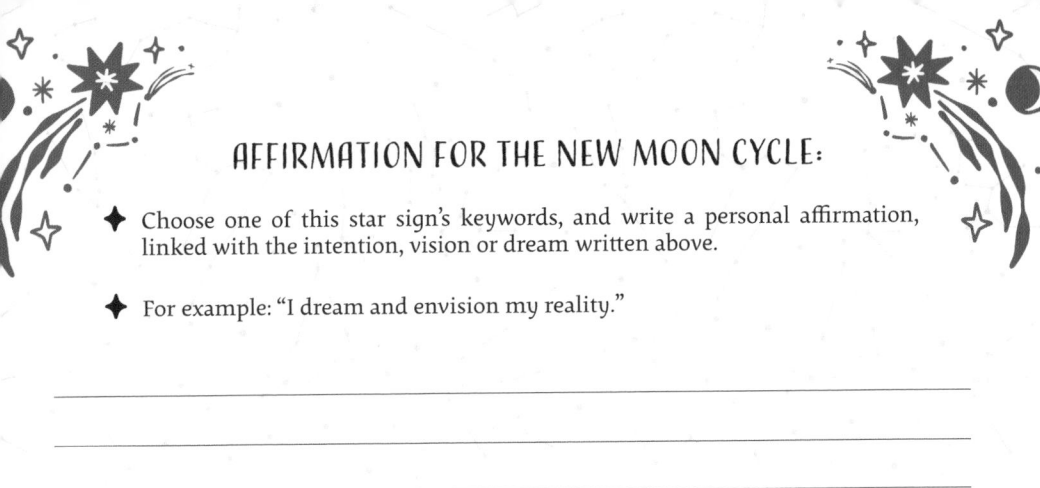

AFFIRMATION FOR THE NEW MOON CYCLE:

✦ Choose one of this star sign's keywords, and write a personal affirmation, linked with the intention, vision or dream written above.

✦ For example: "I dream and envision my reality."

_____

_____

_____

_____

JOURNAL PROMPTS AND SOUL QUESTIONS:

1. Reflection – Select one of the keywords; what does it mean to you? What emotions does it bring up? Choose the word that resonates most by attracting or repelling you. Journal on the meaning of that word: what does it represent to you, how do you see it manifested in the world around you, and how do you express it in your life? Plant your positive seeds at the New Moon and keep that keyword, your reaction to it and your affirmation, in mind during the coming cycle. This will help you to focus on the energy that you wish to manifest or embody in your life.

2. Dreams – Take time to dive into your dreams and allow yourself time to simply be away with the fairies. Do you own a dream diary? This month, try writing down your dreams, and as you retell their stories, reflect on the motifs and themes. What is your subconscious trying to communicate to you? Take time to sit with the paradoxes and absurdity of your inner world, and you might glimpse the reflection of reality.

3. Retreat – Give yourself the opportunity to withdraw from daily life and spend time with yourself. This might be a long break away somewhere or a couple of hours in the evening without your phone. Spend intentional time deepening your spirituality, practicing meditation, or being creative through writing, painting or composing. How does removing outside noise from social media, phones and people around you impact your inner wellbeing? Are you comfortable being by yourself, or does that create anxiety? Practice mindful awareness and journal on your thoughts and emotions.

JOURNAL ON THE NEW MOON

Note down your reflections on the archetype, thoughts from meditation, and answers to the journaling questions.

FULL MOON IN PISCES

The Full Moon in Pisces brings energy into our dreams and visions. If we are willing to listen to our inner voice and open ourselves to possibilities, we can celebrate intuitive insights and healing breakthroughs. As with every archetype, there is a shadow side to Pisces, and with the light of the Full Moon, we can see the tension between our dreams and daily life, which can push us into escapism. A lack of healthy boundaries can expose our heightened sensitivity, which in turn can cause us suffering. The light of Luna can also help us understand the difference between being a mystic or a martyr in our own life.

Record the details of this Full Moon, including which house the Moon is transiting through in your birth chart (if you have it).

Date: Sign degree: House placement:

_____

_____

_____

Write down what you are grateful for, what is blossoming in your life, or what you want to release and let go of at the height of this cycle.

_____

_____

_____

_____

_____

_____

_____

_____

_____

AFFIRMATION FOR THE FULL MOON CYCLE:

✦ Choose a keyword and write a personal affirmation for what you want to release from your life, what you want to let go of or what you want to forgive yourself for, based on the archetypal energy.

✦ For example: "I am grateful for my vivid spiritual world. I release any addictions in my life."

_____

_____

_____

JOURNAL PROMPTS AND SOUL QUESTIONS:

1. Celebration and gratitude – Select one of the keywords and celebrate that feeling or trait in your life. Gratitude is a powerful emotion, helping us maintain our state of physical and emotional wellbeing. By practicing thankfulness on each Full Moon, you're getting into a rhythm of visualizing your dreams on the New Moon and expressing those dreams outwardly on the Full Moon. You can use the idea of celebration and gratitude as a journaling prompt: consider how your chosen keyword manifests in your life. Then, think about how you can celebrate this keyword more. Being mindful and aware of those blessings in your life will, in time, open your mind, so you can see even more things to be grateful for.

2. Escapism – Bring mindful awareness into all the activities in your life that can be considered escapism. Drugs and alcohol are the most well-known, but we can use work or relationships as escapism too. Where in your life do you feel exposed, and what are you trying to hide from? What tricks are you using to disappear? Use the energy of the Full Moon to forgive yourself for not reinforcing your boundaries. Set an intention to find healthy, creative ways to establish time and space for yourself.

3. Victimhood – It's never fun to be victimized, but sometimes we can languish in our own sense of victimization. Have you ever felt so bruised by the world that you wallowed in your hurt, leading you to disassociate from your body or your daily routine? Instead of using this victimhood as an excuse or crutch, what are some ways you could practice self-care and self-love to feel whole again? Use this cycle as an opportunity to let go of negative patterns, forgive yourself and embrace your sensitivity as strength.

JOURNAL ON THE FULL MOON

Here's some space for you to write about all these themes, from practicing gratitude to shadow work.

PREVIOUS NEW MOON IN PISCES

It can help to look back and reflect on where you were emotionally the last time there was a New Moon in Pisces. This reflection can give you some perspective on where you are now. What has changed since then? Did you follow through on the intentions you set at that part of the cycle?

Date: **House placement:**

Reflection on the beginning of the cycle:

_____

_____

_____

_____

_____

_____

_____

_____

_____

_____

_____

_____

_____

_____

_____

_____

_____

_____

_____

_____

_____

_____

VOL III

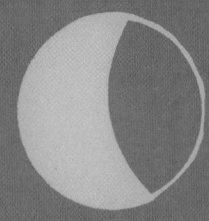

Welcome to the part of the journal that is your reference point and your support system.

If you wish to go deeper, the following chapters provide additional information about the Moon cycle and your personal rhythm.

Beginning an adventure with this journal is like getting to know someone. At first, we can only observe the external stuff – how someone looks, how they are dressed, how they behave. Getting to know Luna and all her phases, her influence and connection with your soul, is like getting to know a friend. It takes time, commitment and attention, but the reward is a beautiful, personal and unique relationship with the cosmos.

MANSIONS IN THE SKY

The zodiac wheel is a symbolic representation of the journey of the Sun through the sky, traveling over the course of the year through 12 starry constellations. In western astrology, the Sun transits through Aquarius in February, visits Cancer in June, and, during Halloween time, shines in Scorpio. In the previous chapter, we got to know each of those archetypes intimately, as we journey with the Moon through the Wheel.

The astrological houses, poetically called "mansions in the sky," divide the heavens into 12 different sections, but they are not linked with the Sun's journey. Houses are based on the Earth's daily rotation, and as she spins on her axis, different constellations rise and set on the horizon. Houses in our personal birth chart show us a snapshot of where in relation to Earth those constellations were located when we were born. For example, your Ascendant, or first house, relates to the constellation that was rising on the eastern horizon at the moment of your birth. The exact time of birth is essential to discover your unique house/zodiac pairing.

You can find out your Ascendant by creating your natal chart on one of many free websites (guidance in appendix). Your Ascendant marks the cusp of your first house, so from there you can follow the constellations anticlockwise to find what sign your other houses fall into. So, if your Ascendant and first house is Leo, then your second house is Virgo, your third house is Libra, and so on. To find out which house the Moon is currently moving through, you need to generate a natal chart "with transits," and then just look for the Moon symbol.

The houses add another layer of information when you use astrology for introspection. While the zodiac signs tell us about the specific archetypal energy that is present, the houses reveal in which area of life that energy will be active. For example, pragmatic Capricorn teaches us about the need to take responsibility and to be accountable for our actions. Houses will tell us if this energy will manifest in the second house of finances, meaning you would need to be mindful of fiscal responsibility; if this energy will manifest in the seventh house of relationships, meaning that responsibility is something you value in your connections; or if it's in the ninth house of philosophy, meaning your beliefs are pragmatic and sometimes rigid. Working with the Moon in Capricorn, we can explore this energy and reflect on how we take responsibility in our life, setting specific intentions for the month or expressing gratitude for the hard work. When we know which of our personal houses is linked with Capricorn, we can tell in which specific area of life this energy is concentrated, which in turn will make our New Moon intentions and Full Moon gratitudes even more focused.

From our self-esteem to our possessions, communication abilities, daily habits, shared resources and reputation, each astrological house can tell us about the aspect of our life that is prominent at the time of a New or Full Moon – and we can add this additional insight into our journaling in the previous section.

HOUSES AND THEIR DOMAINS

As Luna makes her journey throughout the month, she will visit each and every one of the 12 mansions, and will therefore shine her light into different aspects of our everyday life. It's incredibly revealing to follow her path and observe how, every two to three days, our mood changes as the Moon draws us like the tide to different areas of our existence. By observing our physical and emotional responses while paying attention to the Moon's journey, we can learn a lot about our connection with her — yet a busy schedule makes it difficult to notice those subtle shifts.

As this journal helps you to reflect on the New and Full Moon, over time your notes will reveal the connection between the Moon cycle and your own life. You may be surprised to discover how our external and internal energies are connected. But don't take my word for it: just give those exercises a try and you will be astonished at how in tune we are with the world around us.

FIRST HOUSE

KEYWORDS:

+ Will
+ First impression
+ Style
+ Physical appearance
+ Personality
+ Identity
+ Approach to life
+ Self-image
+ How we're perceived
+ Self-interest
+ Initiating action
+ Life force

The first house is all about first impressions, in every meaning of the phrase: how we look, how we dress, what our body type is – everything people see when they first encounter us. This house is not only about the external factors, but also our personality. What is the spark that drives us forward? What temperament do we possess, and how does it help us assert our boundaries and demonstrate who we are? This is also the house of our life force and general health condition. When we meet people face-to-face, they will see our first house.

New Moon in the First House

This is the beginning of a monthly cycle that will concentrate on your self-image. It's time to start something new, perhaps by exploring your identity, physical vitality, or life spirit. On this New Moon, you might want to set an intention to rebrand yourself. Is it time for changes? Your physical appearance tells others a story about who you are as a person, so maybe this month you could reflect on whether your internal self-image matches your external appearance. Why not experiment with new forms of self-expression? If you usually go natural, you could play around with brightly colored makeup; if your clothes are quite modern, maybe try wearing something retro... Something unexpected might bring out your inner spirit for all to see!

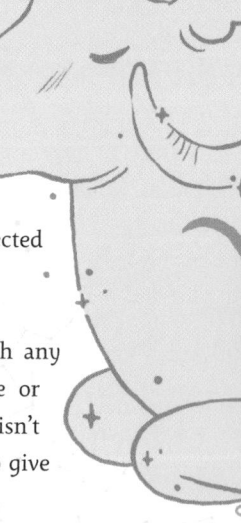

This cycle gives you the opportunity to take action with any personality or character trait that you'd like to change or accentuate. If you view yourself in a certain way that isn't reflected in how others see you, maybe it's time to give that first house a spring clean. The New Moon in this house can help us harmonize our external form with internal character.

Full Moon in the First House

For the next two weeks, this high energy can fuel our emotions in relation to our self-image. This might inflate our self-esteem or give rise to anger. On this Full Moon, work on letting go of other people's perceptions of you, as this can be disadvantageous to the balance of your own self-perception. "What others think about you is none of your business," can be an effective mantra for releasing damaging opinions about your image or character. It's also a good time to let go of personality traits that no longer serve you or are actively harmful to your health. Is your focus on yourself impacting your relationships? If so, then you could use that Full Moon energy to burn out the self-obsession and establish a more balanced approach. If you are struggling with self-image, you can use the Full Moon's energy to highlight your personality, finding a way to express yourself through your appearance and bringing your true self into the limelight. Invite the light of the Full Moon to shine on all your beautiful qualities and celebrate them with others. Be in your fullness, like the Moon, and let your personality shine bright.

SECOND HOUSE

The second house in the horoscope represents our material possessions, our resources, our finances and where they come from. This house can show us what we have and how we've obtained it. What is your attitude towards money? Are you generous and give away what you have, or are you holding onto it and saving for the future? Through money, we can also learn about our internal values, as we tend to spend our money on what we value the most. The second house is also linked to food and the way we nourish our bodies: what we consume and how we consume it. Do you eat quickly, just to sustain yourself, or take your time to enjoy the meal? The Moon cycle in the second house can help us get more in tune with our possessions, our bodies, and our inner values.

KEYWORDS:

+ Values
+ Money
+ Material possessions
+ Self-worth
+ Security needs
+ Nature
+ The five senses
+ Belongings

New Moon in the Second House

A New Moon cycle that begins in the second house will help us concentrate on our assets – our money and our possessions. You can use the new energy of the Moon to plan your finances, or to set a goal for more resources to come into your life. It's also a good time to review your attitude towards money and what, to you, represents worth. What we spend money on can tell us about our own sense of worth – do we treat ourselves to beautiful things because we feel we deserve it? Or do we spend money to "fix" perceived issues in ourselves because we lack self-confidence or a sense of desirability? This New Moon cycle is where you can explore this idea and re-evaluate your relationship with money, possessions, and your sense of self-worth.

Full Moon in the Second House

When the Moon is full in the second house, you have an opportunity to release any tension around money. It can be healthy to be attached to your house and the possessions that make it homely. However, when the attachment turns into an obsession with your belongings, then you may encounter friction. Do you own things, or do they own you? The Full Moon in the second house gives us the opportunity to work with the energy of possessiveness and let go of that which no longer has value. This is also the time to express gratitude for all the resources we value in our lives, and the internal worth that we can see within.

THIRD HOUSE

KEYWORDS:

- ✦ Communication
- ✦ Siblings
- ✦ Neighbors
- ✦ Activity
- ✦ Interests
- ✦ Talents
- ✦ Early education
- ✦ Thinking
- ✦ Short trips
- ✦ Mind
- ✦ Environment

This house represents our siblings and neighborhood, which means those people who are close to us and those who we encounter on a day-to-day basis. This is the house of early learning, which concentrates so much on our communication skills – learning to speak and write is the first formalized teaching that we get. We are taught how to speak and write so that we can convey our ideas to others. With all that activity, it's no wonder this house also tells us about the short trips we're taking. Those are not the dream holidays in Bora Bora, but the short trips we make on a daily basis– trips to work, to the supermarket or to our piano lessons. Any scheduled or regular travel falls under this house.

New Moon in the Third House

This can be a really exciting time in the monthly cycle, as the third house brings a lot of energy and movement into our lives. It's a great time to reflect on the way we communicate and express our minds. Are we clear and precise in our delivery, or are we tangled in our words and thoughts? This is the month to work on how you convey messages to others so that you are understood. During this lunation, we can plant new ideas and work throughout the cycle to convey them clearly. We can dedicate this month to revising, reflecting on or strengthening the bond with our siblings, or with people we consider to be like brothers or sisters to us. This cycle can also help us change and improve our environment. It's a perfect opportunity to get involved in neighborhood activities, or go on some trips around your area to really discover what's hidden around the corner...

Full Moon in the Third House

The Full Moon in the third house helps us express gratitude for our siblings, people we consider as siblings, our close environment and our neighborhood. The heightened energy of the Full Moon can also bring tension in all those areas. Our miscommunications can create arguments with our communities. We might be triggered by those who think in different ways or have different philosophies. This can highlight the lack of information we have gathered, so we cannot make an informed call.

FOURTH HOUSE

KEYWORDS:

- ✦ Home
- ✦ Property
- ✦ Roots
- ✦ Family
- ✦ Ancestry
- ✦ Mother
- ✦ Foundations
- ✦ Early years
- ✦ Conditioning

The fourth house describes your home environment, both in terms of where you actually live and the people you live with. This house talks about our private environment, the most hidden, intimate and personal. It represents our foundation in life. In a material way, this can mean both our childhood home and the home we create for ourselves as an adult. On an emotional level, this is the conditioning we received through our family or caretakers. This is a place of retreat when we need to feel safe and secure. The fourth house represents our roots in terms of ancestry and cultural upbringing, but also the strong foundations that we all require so we can feel safe enough to face the world.

New Moon in the Fourth House

The New Moon in the fourth house begins a cycle that will revolve around our home life. What is home to us? We all came from different backgrounds, but we also have the ability to create a home for ourselves. What lessons from your family home do you want to build on? This Moon cycle might be a great time to reflect on that and plant seeds of change. Maybe you can create some of your own family traditions to help you bond together. This is an ideal month to spend time with your loved ones and really appreciate their company. Go deeper into your roots and reflect on those who came before you and explore the impact they still have on your life. This cycle also invites us to review our foundation and reflect on how we need to grow in order to strengthen our sense of stability and security – both physically, in the house (do we need to schedule repairs or finally redecorate that bedroom?), and emotionally. Do we have enough stability in our lives so that we can go out into the world and not be shaken? Can we build a strong, secure foundation this month to help us cope with others and the world around us?

Full Moon in the Fourth House

When the Full Moon appears in the fourth house, she's bringing to light the shadows of our home life. Luna brings strong energies into our most private environment and asks us to look deeper. If there is friction in our home, can we take accountability instead of getting emotional and hurt? Does our home life suffer as a consequence of our own personal needs, relationships or demands from work? The Full Moon offers the opportunity to release any discordant energy that brings chaos into our safe haven, although we need to be careful not to be overwhelmed by emotions. Luna's energy can also help us celebrate our roots. It's a great time to expand our gratitude for the strong foundations that support our work in the world. It's also a good opportunity to forgive and let go of any family conditioning that is no longer nourishing to us and our souls.

FIFTH HOUSE

The fifth house represents fun and enjoyment of life. This house is traditionally linked with sex and children, but most of all, this is the house of pure creative potential. Here, creativity is not linked specifically to writing or the arts but is expressed in a wider context of making something new – something that lives through us and brings us joy. Whether it is a new dress that we've sewn, a painting that we've created, a bakery that we've opened or a playgroup that we've set up in the local park, the fifth house represents the potential that we see in the ordinary. This is the house of pleasure, self-expression and pure joy.

New Moon in the Fifth House

What brings you joy in life? This is a great question to ask yourself during the New Moon in the fifth house, as this cycle can help you rediscover that joy. If you aren't sure, then ask yourself: what did you enjoy when you were five years old? Was it dancing? Or having imaginary tea parties? Climbing trees? Whatever it was, try to elevate it and bring it into your adult life. Maybe start a dance class, or host a tea ceremony with friends, or begin a mountaineering course! Imagine your five-year-old self being joyful to bring that feeling back into focus. This is the cycle that can help you fall in love with life all over again.

Full Moon in the Fifth House

The Full Moon can bring tension between you and your friends.
Are you a star in your circle, or just a drama queen? Being in the spotlight is wonderful for our self-esteem and can bring out the warm and caring side in us – but it can also cast a shadow where we only see our own greatness and do not see that of others. The Full Moon invites you to evaluate this for yourself, before life evaluates it for you and brings you crashing down from your pedestal. The Full Moon in the fifth house signals a time to celebrate joy and spread happiness. It might be a good time to throw a party – but watch out for the compulsion to be the center of attention. Allow others their time in the Sun, too.

SIXTH HOUSE

The sixth house is traditionally one of health and daily routine, and with good reason. This house is linked with our work – not in terms of our career or what we want to be known for in the world, but in terms of our day-to-day duties. What do you do on a daily basis? Are you an accountant or an artist? Whether you are driving a bus or raising children, your schedule will fall under this house. This mansion also tells us about our health. It's not difficult to draw a connection between health and lifestyle. A daily regimen can either help you stay fit or create issues with your body due to stress, bad diet or sedentary lifestyle. No one is surprised to learn that our daily habits and routines have an incredible impact on our life, and the sixth house reflects that.

KEYWORDS:

- ✦ Health
- ✦ Daily habits
- ✦ Work routine
- ✦ Small pets
- ✦ Illness
- ✦ Injuries
- ✦ Work
- ✦ Service to others

New Moon in the Sixth House

When we want to change our routine and get healthier, the New Moon in the sixth house is a great place to start. This is the Moon cycle to address your underlying health issues and make adjustments to support your recovery. On this New Moon, we can start eating healthier or begin an exercise program that will support our everyday lifestyle and not just further our fitness level. In the sixth house, we have the opportunity to change our everyday behavior, rather than achieving one-time goals (that's a first house matter).

Full Moon in the Sixth House

Full Moon energies in the sixth house can bring to light

any issues with discernment and boundaries. Luna is visiting this mansion in all her glory when she wants to highlight the lack of spiritual or emotional life in our day-to-day schedules. Our lives are not all about work and being healthy, but also about grander meaning; when this is lost, issues around mental health and emotional imbalances might occur. The Full Moon in the sixth house invites us to see our day-to-day routine in a new light, and bring gratitude and awareness to all those small, seemingly insignificant things that make our lives special.

SEVENTH HOUSE

KEYWORDS:

+ Relationships
+ Marriage
+ Contracts
+ Equality
+ Intimate relationships
  (partners, business partners)
+ Open enemies

We learn about ourselves through others. It is when we see ourselves reflected in other people's eyes, in their opinions, in their actions, that we can understand ourselves more fully. The seventh house represents all those one-to-one relationships that have an intimate impact on us: our friendships, marriages and partnerships, our business connections and, yes, enemies too. This is the place of our shadow and all the things that we project onto others. The seventh house is like a house of mirrors, in which others reflect our own fears, insecurities and shortcomings. All those who irritate us beyond rationality, and those that we overreact to, will reveal what we are trying to hide or what we personally struggle with. If we stop and reflect, these irritating people can be our greatest teachers.

We project a lot of our shadow onto close relationships, but we also project our greatness and creativity, our inner light. If we don't feel capable of holding those wonderful attributes, we will see them in people around us, admiring them, envying them and secretly wishing to be them. By looking into the mirror of the seventh house, we can start taking back those projections and integrate them into our lives, to take back the fear and to increase our light.

New Moon in the Seventh House

The New Moon in the seventh house gives us the opportunity to think about people who are closest to us, with whom we have personal, intimate relationships (romantic partners, best friends, business partners, etc.). In this cycle, we can plant the seed of a new relationship or foster the growth of current partnerships. We can also reflect on anyone we have an unnatural aversion to, or those who we admire. Within this cycle, we can then work to integrate our shadow. We can also work to uncover the beauty, creativity, strength and all the other qualities that we are too shy to acknowledge in ourselves.

Full Moon in the Seventh House

The Full Moon in the seventh house is a time of gratitude and celebration of relationships: those close partnerships that challenge us, support us, reflect our greatness back at us and help us face our own fears. This lunation can also highlight issues around individual freedom versus the needs of a relationship. Can you express your own individual energy within a relationship, or are you hiding parts of yourself because you think that's what's best for the dynamic? Does your relationship help and support your own personal development, or is it keeping you shackled to the "old you"? Is "you've changed" an accusation or a compliment? What aspect of the relationship is the Full Moon's light illuminating, and what shadows is it revealing?

EIGHTH HOUSE

After the house of relationships, we enter the house of shared resources. The eighth house is where we share our assets (our money, taxes, house, business assets etc.) with another (partner, business partner, family, bank). This is also a house of deep transformation, a house of hidden things that are not easily seen from the perspective of the first house (of our personality and ego). This is where we are expected to be naked in our truth (no hiding taxes or emotions!) and authenticity. This house invites us to strip away pretense, remove the masks we're hiding behind and share with others what's most valuable to us.

The eighth house generates a lot of fear, as being open and vulnerable happens only when we push through the fear of being seen. This is also the place of sexuality; there is no true union of mind and body without vulnerability and honesty as we strip naked (physically and metaphorically speaking) to expose our most authentic self.

New Moon in the Eighth House

The New Moon in the eighth house helps us reflect on our resources and how we use them. Power and powerlessness can be part of this cycle, as we use our resources (financial, emotional, psychological or spiritual) to consciously or unconsciously manipulate others. This lunation helps us start a journey with our vulnerability, through which we can rediscover our true power and strength. As this is the house of sex, a new cycle can show us what role this plays in our lives. Is it a tool for manipulation in an ongoing power dynamic? Is it how we get closer and more intimate with someone? This period can help us delve deep, really deep, into one of our most intimate encounters and explore the energies that drive us. Power dynamics appear not only in sex but also with money, so this is a good cycle to bring a fresh, thorough approach to our finances, concentrating on paying off debts and credit cards as well as our taxes. By journeying into our money mindset, we can reflect on what power our finances hold over us — or what power we hold over others using our resources.

Full Moon in the Eighth House

When the Moon shines bright in the eighth

house, we can express our gratitude for all the resources we have shared with others, or that have been shared with us... As the light of Luna shines in this house, it can also highlight personal wounds and sore spots around codependency and power struggles. Where in relationships do you give your power away? Who in your life holds power over you, who do you hold onto, and whose resources are you dependent upon (parents, family inheritance, partner's income, etc.)? The eighth house brings questions around those themes and helps us be grateful for the support that we have. It is the perfect time to reflect on those bonds that no longer serve us, that hold us in a position of disempowerment, that make us feel dependent. See them in a different light and release anything that is no longer of value. What relationship dynamics are making you feel undervalued? Are there any resources in your life that you do not believe are being shared fairly?

NINTH HOUSE

The ninth house invites us to take a journey. This could be physical – through different countries, cultures, landscapes – or metaphorical, through books, poetry, documentaries and different viewpoints. In this mansion, we solidify and expand our philosophy of life by interacting with foreign people, cultures, and thoughts. We get to know various approaches to life through doctrines, ideology or religion. We explore fairy tales and folklore to understand the archetypes that guide our lives, and in following this journey, we come to a place where we feel comfortable – where we can better understand both the world and our own life. This is where we uncover the story that we'll be sharing with others. It's a place where we develop our personal doctrine that resonates with our most authentic self. It's the wisdom of our life that directs any decision, and our own life's purpose. This is the house that reveals the convictions that inform our choices, the internal law that is externalized each time we use it to make a judgement.

KEYWORDS:

+ Travel
+ Philosophy
+ Higher education
+ Law
+ Religion
+ Different cultures
+ Learning
+ Ethics
+ Divination
+ Magic
+ Temples
+ Astrology
+ Foreigners
+ Pilgrimage (a religious or spiritual journey)

New Moon in the Ninth House

When the New Moon cycle starts in our ninth house, we have the opportunity to travel and learn. We can plan our once-in-a-lifetime trip, or we can take on a new course and attend classes on an interesting subject. Whichever route we take, this is the month of exploration. It's a new cycle of following our own story and asking ourselves if this is the meaning we want for our lives, or if we want to rewrite our own adventure. This is a great time to ask ourselves questions about whether our judgement calls come from our own experience, or from gossip and other people's opinions.

Full Moon in the Ninth House

With the light of the Full Moon shining in the ninth house, we can express gratitude for the freedom in our life. Freedom to travel, to think, to learn, to speak up, to make our own decisions and think for ourselves. This is hard-won freedom and not given to many, yet so many who have it take it for granted. Take time to acknowledge how you enjoy this freedom, and journal your feelings of gratitude. This is the time when your explorations bear fruit, so appreciate how far you've travelled. The Full Moon can also highlight the polarity of sharing information for the purpose of deepening our understanding versus sharing information that does not bring value into our lives. Of the content that you consume, what is worth your energy? Does sharing gossip, fake or unconfirmed information enrich your life, or does it only create drama and spread anxiety? The Full Moon will bring to light any issues with truthfulness. Take responsibility for the stories you share.

TENTH HOUSE

KEYWORDS:

+ Career
+ Social standing
+ Goals
+ Mastery
+ Reputation
+ Public image
+ Authority
+ Vocation

Traditionally known as the house of "public image," this is the space where you are seen by the world. If someone were to Google your name, the information they would find about you resonates with the tenth house. For most, this is the house of career, as this is what they've chosen to build in the world, but this house can represent so much more. In the tenth house, we respond to our calling and take all that we are – our foundations, our talents, our joy and creativity – and we learn how to master it to build something for the society that we live in. No man is an

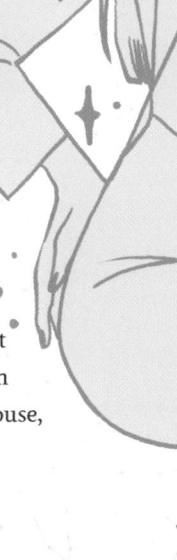

island, and the tenth house shows our footprint on both our culture and the world at large. This is the house of mastery of chosen subjects. Whether you've chosen to be a stay-at-home mom and raise your children, build a company from the ground up or become an artist with a nomadic lifestyle, any choice of yours requires mastery of skills, building strong foundations and putting yourself out in the world. Even counter-cultural work, like campaigning to revolutionize societal structures, is still contributing, as opposing voices are needed in the healthy development and growth of any society. The tenth house is where you can master your talents, stand out, and make a change in a way that is unique to you.

New Moon in the Tenth House

New beginnings in the tenth house can help plant seeds of new job and career adventures. When the New Moon transits through the tenth house, this is a great time to visualize future growth in your chosen field of work, or to develop vital skills for career progression. Remember that success means different things to different people, so this is the opportune moment to meditate on what success means to you. Define that success and build the foundation you need to achieve it. You can channel the energy of the tenth house into a new beginning that will lead to you mastering the skills you need to follow your calling. This mansion, like no other, shows us the value of personal accountability. If we want something but we're not prepared to put work into it and be consistent, then we cannot blame anyone else for our lack of success.

Full Moon in the Tenth House

Luna will highlight this house and bring energy to celebrate our success in the world. She will illuminate everything that we are proud of achieving and that we're happy to share with the world around us. This is a wonderful time to celebrate the fruits of our labor. As the Full Moon enters this house, she will shine light onto our achievements – but under this light, we won't be able to hide any shortcomings, either. If there is anything that we've worked on that has been built on shaky foundations, if it is not well rooted or has overshadowed our family life or self-nourishment, the tension between our outer and inner worlds might come to the surface.

ELEVENTH HOUSE

KEYWORDS:

+ Friends
+ Associates
+ Groups
+ Social groups
+ Hopes
+ Wishes
+ Friendships
+ Acquaintances

The eleventh house is that of hopes and dreams, also known as the house of good fortune, and as such, it's a bit trickier to define. This house tells us about the aspirations that we hold in our hearts: what would bring us joy and fulfilment, what we want to create, what causes we hold most dear. Here, we meet others who have similar interests and share our vision, whether it's getting involved in animal welfare, political activism, climbing mountains, dancing salsa or crocheting together. This is the place where we connect with friends who share our hopes and dreams, a place of connections forged from shared interests.

New Moon in the Eleventh House

The new cycle that begins in the eleventh house is a particularly good time to create a vision board. This New Moon will help you reflect on your dreams and plant seeds so they can grow. However, it's wise to remember that old saying: "Be careful what you wish for because it might come true." This fairy tale warning is as valid in Disney stories as it is in our lives. For our wishes to fulfil our heart's desire, they must be rooted in our soul's calling. Otherwise, a dream can turn into a nightmare when a long-awaited solution is not what we really wanted. This month, take time to really ask your heart what it truly desires and listen to the answer. Then, put those dreams on a board, in a journal or speak them out loud, so the universe can work with you to manifest them.

Full Moon in the Eleventh House

When the light of the Full Moon brightens the eleventh house, we celebrate our wish's fulfilment. Make a list of all the wishes that you planted at the last New Moon of this monthly cycle, the last New Moon in this sign, or the general wishes that have been fulfilled in your life and celebrate them with gratitude and joy. So often in life we strive for more: to go further, climb higher, dive deeper, and we do not stop to see what we've already achieved. The eleventh house, in the spotlight of the Full Moon, helps us clearly see the beautiful magic of dreams fulfilled. Even if they seem small, insignificant or childish, they are still full of wonder and universal fairy dust. Acknowledge them and be grateful. The energy of Luna in this house can also show us the heartache of wishes unfulfilled or dreams unacknowledged. Where in your life do you hide your dreams? What joys and hopes do you deny yourself in fear that they might come true and overwhelm you — so you play it safe and small instead? In the light of the Moon, look at all the dreams you've outgrown and must let go of, but also at the hopes that you hide even from yourself.

TWELFTH HOUSE

The most mysterious and feared house in astrology, this is the place of the unknown and unconscious, the two most feared concepts from the perspective of our ego. The first house is all about who we are, our appearance, our character, our individuality and how different we are from "the other." In the twelfth house, all that falls away and we meet with the collective, which can be overwhelming and scary. Here, we encounter things bigger than we are, bigger than our individual ego can handle. We meet with the divine and have spiritual experiences that take us away from our everyday life, to the realm of the gods. This house is where we take a spiritual or meditative retreat. In solitude, we face our inner life, confront our inner demons and commune with our inner angels. In the twelfth house, we can meet our spiritual self, but it is also the house that finds us trying to escape reality through the use of drugs or alcohol. These intoxicants dissolve our current reality, and while we are under their influence we are transported to a different realm, away from pain and suffering. We try to heal in the twelfth house, and we tend to do that in isolation, voluntarily or otherwise. As this placement opposes the sixth house, which is the house of physical health, it also tells us about the connection between body and mind. When our body suffers so does our mental health, and this works in reverse too. Here, we can try to heal both. This is where we link

KEYWORDS:

- Hidden enemies
- Confinement
- Hospitals
- Prisons
- Monasteries
- Retreats
- Release
- Unconscious
- Suffering
- Illness
- Deconstruction

with the collective unconscious to bridge the gap between reality and dreams, between the individual path and a calling. Artists, activists, musicians, politicians and anyone who has a strong connection to a collective undercurrent will express the needs of the many through their individual paths.

New Moon in the Twelfth House

With a new cycle starting in this house, you have a month to reconnect with something bigger than yourself. It's your time to start a spiritual practice like meditation or go on a spiritual retreat to reconnect with your inner world. It's a beautiful time of planting seeds of devotion. This is also the perfect opportunity to work behind the scenes on a project that requires time in isolation, that requires you to commune with your intuition or with collective desires, with inspiration and muses. As this is the house of self-undoing, the New Moon cycle invites you to reflect on all the things that you might unconsciously be doing that are unraveling your plans. Spend some time journaling on things you cannot see: your blind spots and situations that make you want to retreat instead of responding. This month, you can intuit what archetype is at play in your life that you need to pay more attention to.

Full Moon in the Twelfth House

The Full Moon in this house might bring intense emotions. As you are in the realm of the collective, you might be feeling the emotions of everyone around you. Stay grounded in your everyday routine and in your body to help maintain balance between your intuition and external stimuli. In the full light of the Moon, you can also see all the tension between your everyday routines and habits (sixth house), how they relate to your spiritual life and mental health, and how they are working in the service of the collective. The Full Moon in this house can also bring to light our secrets, whether they are long-buried family secrets or untold stories, unexpressed emotions or uncommunicated desires. This is the cycle to look at all that's hidden and work with it, so that the energy it takes to keep things secret will no longer drain us and prevent us from enjoying our daily life.

YOUR PERSONAL MOON

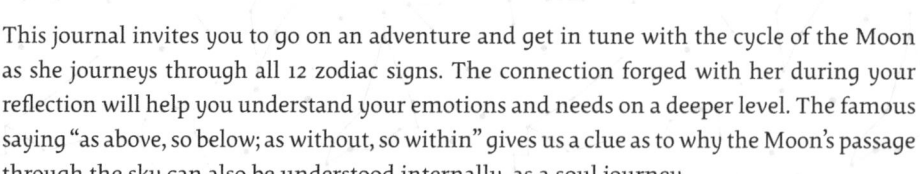

This journal invites you to go on an adventure and get in tune with the cycle of the Moon as she journeys through all 12 zodiac signs. The connection forged with her during your reflection will help you understand your emotions and needs on a deeper level. The famous saying "as above, so below; as without, so within" gives us a clue as to why the Moon's passage through the sky can also be understood internally, as a soul journey.

This part of the book is not linked with journaling, but is rather a sort of bonus content to introduce you to the astrological Moon, your birth chart Moon phase and her journey during your lifetime.

When we were born and drew our first breath, the Moon was in one of her eight phases. Her position in the sky at the time of our birth, whether it was a Waxing Crescent, Waning Gibbous or another phase, can give us a deeper understanding of our needs. This will also make us more sensitive when the Moon returns each month to the phase she was in at your birth. You can learn about your personal Moon phase from your birth chart by measuring the degrees between the Sun and Moon's placement. To do this, you count the degrees between Sun and Moon going anticlockwise. This value will help you locate your personal Moon phase and description below. You can also find this information online (website in the appendix) by entering your birth data.

The beauty of Luna is that she can guide us in the heavens above as well as through our internal sky. We can deepen our connection to the Moon energies by following our internal clock, as well.

YOUR PERSONAL MOON PHASE

New Moon 0 – 45 degrees
New Moon types are often subjective, as their emotional life (Moon) is so close to their inner light (Sun) that it's difficult to see anything else. They embrace life with the zest of a newborn and everything is exciting, fresh and full of fiery energy. New Moon people have a seed of a vision and they see the world through the lens of potentiality. As the Sun and the Moon are so close together, this type has a strong need to embody the spiritual essence of their light.

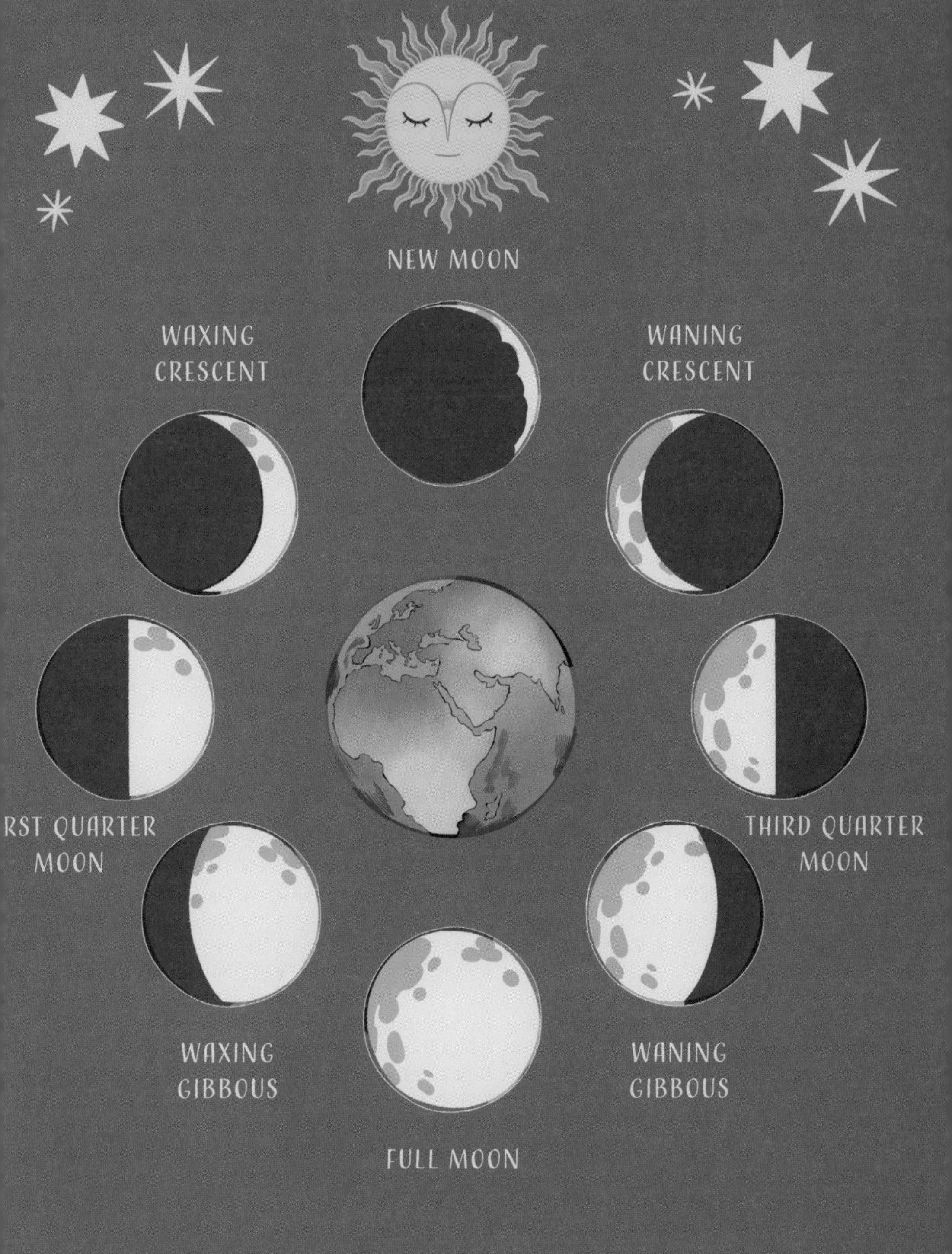

NEW MOON

WAXING
CRESCENT

WANING
CRESCENT

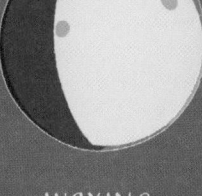

RST QUARTER
MOON

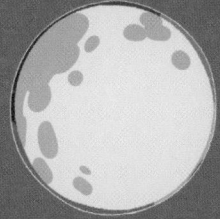

THIRD QUARTER
MOON

WAXING
GIBBOUS

WANING
GIBBOUS

FULL MOON

THE MOON PHASES

Waxing Crescent Moon 45 – 90 degrees

The Waxing Crescent personality is here to take the first step and sprout into action. The seed has been planted and this type is finding the strength to push through and bring it to the light. Their impatience and excitement are palpable, and their creativity is strong, yet this personality carries the heavy weight of the past even as they plant new ideas. They need to learn how to not be ruled by memories so they can introduce new concepts in a more conscious way.

First Quarter Moon 90 – 135 degrees

Traditionally this lunation is called "crisis in action" and those born in this phase have a strong desire to build the groundwork for the ideas planted at the New Moon. The impulsive quality of the Crescent type is not enough: this phase needs commitment and strength to create something solid. These newly constructed systems are needed to help the New Moon impulse grow and flourish, but also to prevent it from being torn down with the old and crumbling structures around it. People with this phase have a strong vision of how to establish new ideas.

Waxing Gibbous Moon 135 – 180 degrees

People born under Waxing Gibbous are so close to the fullness of the cycle that they can taste it. They are committed to growth and development as they seek the light of illumination. As they are so close to the peak of the cycle, they are aware of the journey yet to be taken, but their excitement is still present. However, as they are further away from the idea's New Moon seed, they are somewhat detached from it. This can lead them to be more objective and incorporate new ideas, but might also cause them to lose sight of why they started this journey.

Full Moon 180 – 225 degrees

The Full Moon is the apex of the cycle, and with the light of the Moon shining bright, the seed idea planted at the beginning is illuminated and brought to consciousness. Objectivity in approach replaces the energy of an intuitive path. This type brings to light and embodies the idea planted at the New Moon yet deals with the tension of opposition (as the Sun is opposing the Moon). This means this type can protect their truth but reject anything that opposes it.

Waning Gibbous / Disseminating Moon 225 – 270 degrees

The Disseminating type takes the flourishing of the idea from the Full Moon phase — but without the tension of opposition, they have a chance to share it with others. It's not enough to achieve the peak of the cycle (as in Full Moon type), but there is a need to spread the message, share the idea and communicate what they've learnt with others, even if it means to disseminate the previous notions and structures.

Third Quarter Moon 270 – 315 degrees

Another crisis point in the cycle is known as the "crisis in consciousness." This type is guided by their strong inner beliefs and the vision of the future that they can glimpse, yet no one else can see. To work towards these new ideas (New Moon seed) that they alone can sense takes great inner courage and strength, yet for the new idea to be realized, they also need to learn not to hold on too tightly to idealism, but to let go of any part of this vision that will prevent them from reaching their final goal.

Waning Crescent/Balsamic Moon 315 – 360 degrees

This type is facing the future and preparing the new seed of ideas to be planted at the next New Moon. They are born at the end of the cycle, so the exhaustion of the journey so far — ideas born and completed and dying out — is part of their makeup. Yet they have such a strong sense of the new worlds that could exist that they can become too rigid and fanatical about bringing them about. They know that for a new world to be born, the old has to go down in flames.

THE PROGRESSED MOON: YOUR SOUL'S JOURNEY THROUGH THE PHASES

The beauty of the cosmos is that the sky above is also reflected within you. Just as you were born under a specific Moon phase, which tells us about your emotional needs and conditioned responses, you also have an internal Moon journey which shows the possibility of growth and development. This personal lunar clock is measured by an astrological technique called the Progressed Chart. This reveals how our birth chart changes over the years and how we evolve. This chart moves the Sun one degree a year and the Moon around 12 degrees a year, giving us a glimpse into our soul's internal journey, our changing needs and our emotional growth.

As the Moon moves through various constellations and phases in the sky, so too does she move through these in our internal world, giving us two and a half to three years of a specific sign and phase. The Progressed Chart shows us the two main strands of our path:

Firstly – it shows us the Progressed Moon's 27-year cycle, wherein our Moon goes through all 12 zodiac signs and arrives back at the sign and degree of our birth. The Progressed Moon changes signs every two and a half years, and reveals how our internal mood changes, which zodiac energy is now active in our lives, and which internal house needs our attention and nourishment. Through this inner voyage around the 12 archetypes, we have the opportunity to develop emotional language and maturity.

Secondly – it shows us that we, too, go through an internal version of all eight phases in our lives. Through her journey, as the Progressed Moon makes the connection with the Progressed Sun, we ourselves progress through our personal New Moon, Waxing Crescent, First Quarter, Waxing Gibbous, Full Moon, Waning Gibbous, Third Quarter and a Balsamic phase roughly every three and a half years. This cycle takes approximately 30 years in total and teaches us about our inner world and which part of the cycle we are going through at the time. We will experience the world and life differently depending on whether we are in the closing Balsamic phase of life, or if we are in an expansive and energetic Full Moon phase. It helps us understand the undercurrent of our life and why things might feel more difficult when only a year before they were so much easier.

By understanding our Personal Moon journey through the zodiac, you can gain a deeper understanding of your psychological needs and triggers, your special needs for nourishment and which archetypal energies might be influencing your emotional life. Knowing the inner rhythm of your Personal Moon phase gives you a blueprint of your energy levels; you can connect to the cycle of the Moon to allow yourself to go with the flow, instead of against the current. To view your current Personal Moon path, check the information in your Progressed Chart (info in appendix).

THE PROGRESSED MOON THROUGH THE ZODIAC:

Aries

Our emotional life is instinctual, daring and competitive. We have lots of energy that can, if it is not expressed, turn into anger and rage. We need nourishment through movement, initiating action and experiencing new adventures.

Taurus

Our emotional life slows down, and we have a greater appreciation of our senses and our body. This sense of security is important, and we pay more attention to our personal possessions. We nourish ourselves through contact with the earth, food and our bodies.

Gemini

Our emotional life is buzzing with the excitement of new ideas. We become sociable and inquisitive. Our curiosity prompts us to learn and communicate with our networks. We nourish ourselves by creating connections and exchanging ideas.

Cancer

Our emotional life concentrates on family matters. We become more protective of our homes and our loved ones. We might become aware of early childhood conditioning. We might be more sensitive than usual. We nourish ourselves by spending time with those who make us feel safe and comfortable.

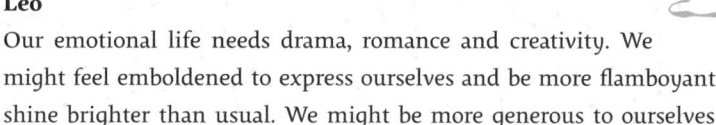

Leo

Our emotional life needs drama, romance and creativity. We might feel emboldened to express ourselves and be more flamboyant and shine brighter than usual. We might be more generous to ourselves and to others. We nourish ourselves by tapping into our creative potential, by getting involved in activities that bring us pure joy and by discovering our inner child's needs.

Virgo

Our emotional life needs discipline and organization. We concentrate more on our health and improve our everyday routines. We might be consumed by the need for perfection and improvement. We nourish ourselves by creating a clear and uncluttered space around us and within.

Libra

Our emotional life might need balance and harmony. We might be more concerned with our appearance. We seek to expand our social circle and crave the company of others. We nourish ourselves through our relationships, and though interacting with art, poetry and other forms of beauty.

Scorpio

Our emotional life takes us to the depth of our raw feelings and deepens our vulnerability. We might face fears that have been buried deep, or confront taboo subjects that are difficult for us. We nourish ourselves through deep and powerful relationships with others, and through a commitment to stay in our own power.

Sagittarius

Our emotional life requires space and freedom. We have a strong need for expansion and new experiences both in the outside world and in our inner world. We nourish ourselves through travel and spending time in the great outdoors, as well as broadening our horizons through new courses and teachers.

Capricorn

Our emotional life needs maturity and structure. We have a strong need for traditional values and commitment to work. We nourish ourselves by attending familiar events, by mastering subjects we're passionate about and receiving recognition for our achievements.

Aquarius

Our emotional life needs independence and freedom of expression. We might be attracted to new and unusual activities, people or events. We are drawn to groups and social circles with rebellious streaks. We nourish ourselves by embracing and expressing our own originality and independence.

Pisces

Our emotional life needs dreams, vision and spirituality. We're experiencing inner longings and are drawn to any form of escapism. We nourish ourselves by retreating and spending time with our soul, by engaging with our dreams and listening to our inner voice of intuition.

PROGRESSED MOON PHASES:

New Moon 0 – 45 degrees

The New Moon phase is the beginning of a new 27-year cycle. It's time to plant new seeds, envision new futures, and plan new adventures. New possibilities are opening up and there is a surge of fresh, uninhibited energy. We might be swept away on a wave of excitement and our actions might be impulsive. This phase is so instinctual that we might not have space for reflection but instead rely only on our instincts.

Waxing Crescent Moon 45 – 90 degrees

The Waxing Crescent phase brings us struggles with stagnation and apathy. These two and a half years will demand that we take action: that we break through limiting beliefs and push forward with courage. We might be very sensitive and struggle with the tasks ahead of us, but this phase also brings excitement every time we overcome obstacles and push towards our goal.

First Quarter Moon 90 – 135 degrees

The First Quarter phase presents us with a crisis in order to force us to make decisions, to stand by the decisions we made at the New Moon phase and to follow through on our plans. We are faced with challenging circumstances that motivate us to step into our power and take control.

Waxing Gibbous Moon 150 – 180 degrees

In the two and a half years before the fullness of the cycle, we are working towards improvements in our lives. We are perfecting all that we have fought hard to build over the past few years, both in our outer and inner worlds. We are also more aware of our work having an impact on others in our community or society.

Full Moon 180 – 225 degrees

It's a time of celebration of how far we've come. We can take this opportunity to look back to the New Moon years, when we planted those seeds that are now growing and blossoming. These couple of years also help us search for the meaning in everything that we've struggled to bring into being. We've worked hard to create this life, so at the Full Moon we ask ourselves: "Why? What was the purpose of all this?"

Waning Gibbous / Disseminating Moon 225 – 270 degrees

The Disseminating phase can help us answer the questions that we explored in the Full Moon phase. This is when the search for meaning and purpose is over, and we are living our dreams on a daily basis. We understand that the fruits of our labors are best shared and enjoyed with others. We spend these couple of years being drawn to groups and people who can connect with our purpose.

Third Quarter Moon 270 – 315 degrees

At the Third Quarter time in our lives, we come to another crisis. After years of pushing through and building the life we've wanted and then enjoying the fruits of that success, we come to a turning point. We are beginning to let go of the dreams and values we held for years. As we have matured, we have come to learn that certain structures and beliefs are too restrictive, and they need to be discarded. At this phase in our lives, we struggle between expectations from others for us to stay the same, and our internal need for transformation.

Waning Crescent/Balsamic Moon 315 – 360 degrees

In the Balsamic Moon of our lives, we are ready to let go, to forgive and forget, to dismantle all that we've learnt in the previous phase that no longer serves us. It's a time of cleansing our lives of all that belongs in the past and has no place in our new future. This is the time of retreat and hibernation, so we can dream new dreams and preserve our strength before the next New Moon phase. The Balsamic phase is a transitory phase that bridges one full 30-year cycle with another, where we decide what wisdom we will take into our future.

FAREWELL

AND HAPPY JOURNEYING!

We've come to the end of our adventure together. I hope you enjoyed this journey and that it brought you a lot of laughter, joy, surprises and breakthroughs — but most importantly, I hope it brought you closer to your inner world. This is just the beginning of a beautiful adventure with your soul and with the world around you through the cycles of growth and transformation.

As with anything in life, this journal has its limitations, therefore all the archetypes and possibilities described here are touching just the tip of the iceberg. The way those energies operate within our own psyche and within the world is limitless. My aim was to introduce you to them and invite you to start your own relationship with them. I hope that you will not cease from exploration and you will get to know a plethora of expressions of those energies in the world.

NOTES

APPENDIX

Here, you can find online resources that will allow you to generate your birth chart. These are free websites, and you can even download your chart to reference later.

Astro-Seek

URL: https://mooncalendar.astro-seek.com/

Navigate to "Free Horoscopes / Birth Natal Chart Calculator Online." Then, enter the date, time and place of your birth. This chart will show your Ascendant and houses, as well as the Moon phase you were born under.

To find your Progressed Moon, navigate to "Free Horoscopes / Secondary Progression / Solar Returns." Select "Prognosis / Secondary Progressions (Secondary Directions)." Enter the date, time and place of your birth. This chart will show the location of your Progressed Moon and Sun.

Astro.com

URL: https://www.astro.com/horoscope

Enter the date, time and place of your birth to generate your birth chart. There are a few charts to choose from. The "Natal Chart Wheel" provides your birth chart and information about houses. The "Progressed Chart" shows the location of your Progressed Moon and Sun. The "House System" chart will show your Ascendant and houses.

GLOSSARY

Archetype
An idea universally present in the human psyche and in storytelling. In astrology, "archetype" is another way to refer to the personas and myths that the 12 zodiac signs were named after.

Cycle
A complete orbit of a celestial body (e.g.: a planet, the Moon, etc.) around the chart or another celestial body.

Element
The concept of classical elements, used in astrology to classify different qualities of the zodiac signs.

Horoscope
A common word in astrology, this can refer to a (usually short range or monthly) astrological forecast for particular signs (e.g.: the horoscope pages in magazines) or, more broadly, to refer to the birth chart.

Houses
The method used by astrologers to divide the birth chart into 12 parts. There are many different house systems in Western astrology. In this book, we refer to the Whole Sign House system, which links each house with each sign of the zodiac, beginning with the Rising Sign.

Luminaries
Also known as The Lights in the horoscope, this term refers to the Moon and the Sun.

Luna
Latin name for the Moon. Can also refer to a Roman goddess of the Moon (sometimes identified as Diana).

Lunation
The period of time from one New Moon to the next New Moon. A lunar month.

Moon phase
The part of the Moon's surface which is illuminated by the Sun and visible from the Earth, which gradually changes over the course of the lunar month.

Natal chart
Otherwise known as your birth chart. Symbolic map of the sky at the time of birth (or any other localized event).

Natal Moon
The position of the Moon in a birth chart (including the sign and house the Moon is located in).

Zodiac Wheel
The apparent path of the Sun across the sky (ecliptic). In astrology, this path is divided into 12 equally measured (30 degree) constellations, which make up the star signs.

ABOUT THE AUTHOR

Monika is a transformational astrologer and a mindfulness coach based in the West Midlands, UK. Originally from Poland, she relocated nearly two decades ago to put down roots and make a home in the UK, which she now shares with her husband and two rescue cats. She has always been fascinated by the language of symbols, fairy tales, archetypes, mythology and the magic they create when woven together – crafting a tapestry of life.

When Monika discovered astrology and experienced the intense power of metamorphosis, she understood she had a beautiful framework to help others on their path of discovery and healing. There is power in storytelling, in our personal mythology and something profoundly transformational in recognizing our own tale, familiarizing ourselves with it, and then glimpsing meaning behind all our trials and tribulations. We may even become empowered to write our own adventure. She feels privileged to be of service and assist others in their journey.

Connect with Monika:
Monika can be found sharing astrology and life on IG @modernyaga as well as on her website: www.modernyaga.com

ABOUT THE ARTIST

Sibylline is a freelance illustrator from France, working as a comic artist, character designer, and illustrator for magazines and books. She has worked in Europe and the US with high-profile clients including Warner Bros, Boom Studios, Netflix, and Hachette. She loves cookies, jasmine tea and drawing girls and animals.

Connect with Sibylline:
Sibylline can be found illustrating on IG @sibylline_m as well as on her website: www.sibyllinemeynet.com